T0300134

ROUTLEDGE LIBRARY EDITIONS: SMALL BUSINESS

Volume 2

BARRIERS TO GROWTH IN SMALL FIRMS

BARRIERS TO GROWTH IN SMALL FIRMS

Edited by
J. BARBER, J.S. METCALFE AND M. PORTEOUS

Routledge
Taylor & Francis Group

LONDON AND NEW YORK

First published in 1989 by Routledge

This edition first published in 2016
by Routledge
2 Park Square, Milton Park, Abingdon, Oxon OX14 4RN

and by Routledge
711 Third Avenue, New York, NY 10017

Routledge is an imprint of the Taylor & Francis Group, an informa business

British Library Cataloguing in Publication Data
A catalogue record for this book is available from the British Library

ISBN: 978-1-138-67308-3 (Set)
ISBN: 978-1-315-54266-9 (Set) (ebk)
ISBN: 978-1-138-67985-6 (Volume 2) (hbk)
ISBN: 978-1-315-56351-0 (Volume 2) (ebk)

Publisher's Note
The publisher has gone to great lengths to ensure the quality of this reprint but
points out that some imperfections in the original copies may be apparent.

Disclaimer
The publisher has made every effort to trace copyright holders and would welcome
correspondence from those they have been unable to trace.

BARRIERS
TO GROWTH
IN SMALL
FIRMS

EDITED BY J.BARBER,
J.S.METCALFE
AND M.PORTEOUS

R

Routledge
London and New York

First published in 1989 by
Routledge
11 New Fetter Lane, London EC4P 4EE
29 West 35th Street, New York NY 10001

British Library Cataloguing in Publication Data

Barriers to growth in small firms. — (Small
    business series).
    1. Great Britain. Small firms. Growth.
    Restriction
    I. Barber, J.   II. Metcalfe, J. Stan
    III. Porteous, M. (Mike)   IV. Series
    338.6'42

    ISBN 0-415-00093-9

Library of Congress Cataloging in Publication Data

Barriers to growth in small firms /
    editors J. Barber, J.S. Metcalfe, M. Porteous.
        p.   cm. — (Small business series)
    Bibliography: p.
    Includes index.
    ISBN 0-415-00093-9
    1. Small business — Growth.   I. Barber, J. (John)
II. Metcalfe, J.S. (J. Stanley)   III. Porteous, M. (Mike)
IV. Series.
HD2341.B27 1989
338.6'42 — dc19

Photoset by Mayhew Typesetting, Bristol, England
Printed in Great Britain by Billing & Sons Ltd, Worcester

Contents

Contributors

John Barber
Economics Division 1, Department of Trade and Industry

Mark Beesley
Science Policy Research Unit, University of Sussex

Derek Bosworth
Institute of Employment Research, University of Warwick

Graham Hall
Manchester Business School

Keith Hartley
Institute for Research in the Social Sciences, University of York

Alan Hughes
Faculty of Economics and Politics, University of Cambridge

John Hutton
Centre for Health Economics, University of York

Chris Jacobs
Institute of Employment Research, University of Warwick

John McGee
Templeton College, Oxford

Stanley Metcalfe
Department of Economics, University of Manchester

Mike Porteous
Research and Technology Policy Division, Department of Trade and Industry

Roy Rothwell
Science Policy Research Unit, University of Sussex

Foreword

In August 1986, ACARD (The Advisory Council for Applied Research and Development) together with the Department of Trade and Industry initiated a study to examine the barriers to growth faced by small, innovative firms in the UK and to propose means by which these might be overcome.

ACARD believed that the growth of small firms is an important contributor to a technically advanced and innovative economy, because in some cases it may be easier for new technologies to be exploited initially through new firms, and also because of the competitive pressure which is applied to established larger firms. ACARD was therefore interested in how small firms, once established, grow into medium size band, a process which often involves a transition from being a narrow-niche producer to a company with a range of products within a particular specialism. Some ACARD members believed that this process is more difficult in the UK than in other industrial economies. The objective of this study is therefore to identify the barriers to growth, and the steps that might be taken to mitigate their effects.

As a first step towards determining how ACARD could contribute to an understanding of the barriers to the growth of small firms, six academic experts were asked to prepare short overview papers, dealing with separate aspects of the problem.

The papers contained in this volume were prepared by the six experts and presented to a Seminar at Rolls Royce PLC in February 1987. They make very interesting reading and enabled ACARD to identify the main lines of enquiry for a further study. Since then, ACARD has been replaced by ACOST (The Advisory Council on Science and Technology) and ACOST has established a study group to take this process of investigation and recommendation further.

ACOST is grateful to the Research and Technology Policy division of DTI who provided the funding for the expert reviews and to the ACARD Secretariat. From the DTI Mr J. Barber and Dr M. Porteous supervised the study with the assistance of a number of rapporteurs from the DTI and Department of Employment. The contributions of Mr Barber and Dr Porteous do not necessarily reflect the official views of the Department of Trade and Industry.

Francis Tombs

Preface

It is almost impossible to be unaware that we live nowadays in an 'enterprise economy' in which those individuals with a spirit of entrepreneurship are rewarded if their efforts are judged to be a success in the market-place.

In almost every developed country since the late 1970s the small firm sector, which best characterises this entrepreneurial spirit, has become a subject of increasing interest. No longer is the small firm viewed as being synonymous with back-street operations eking out a barely satisfactory living for their proprietor and providing low-paid jobs for their workers. Instead, in the last few years, the small firm has become more popularly viewed as a high technology operation and its owner as the modern folk hero.

In many ways it is unfortunate that whilst there has been this rapid shift in the popular (and politicians') view of small firms, the real level of knowledge about such firms is surprisingly low. In most cases the smallest size of firm is not fully included in government statistics, even for the manufacturing sector, whilst the service sector where small firms have been growing most rapidly traditionally is an area of statistical ignorance. Finally the major study of small firms in the UK, under the Chairmanship of John Bolton, was published in 1971 at a time when the major public concern was whether or not the sector was likely to survive. Clearly these are not the issues of today, and yet much of the received wisdom about small firms, even at the end of the 1980s is derived from that study.

It is not unreasonable to say that the flurry of political interest in the small firm sector at the end of the 1970s, and the development of new initiatives for much of the 1980s, was in many cases based upon an imperfect understanding of the factors influencing the birth, death and performance of small firms. At this stage in the

1980s the lacuna is slowly being filled by the emergence of high quality research based upon extensive empirical work.

It is the purpose of the Routledge Small Business Series to include a range of titles which will claim to cover the subject of small business from a range of disciplinary perspectives. The unifying theme of the series will be the question of public policy towards small firms, and so it will not include texts which are concerned with teaching individuals how to become better entrepreneurs.

Given these objectives for the series, the present volume is particularly welcome since it considers a major theme – that of the factors influencing the growth of small firms into medium- and large-sized firms. The importance of this theme is demonstrated by the finding that, in the small firm sector in the UK, approximately half the growth in the sector comes from about 4 per cent of the firms. The remainder of the firms in the sector will either cease to trade over that period or will experience only very modest growth.

A second theme of the book is the high technology sector which is increasingly expected to spawn many of these rapid growth firms. The barriers to growth in such firms may be expected to be of a different nature, or to operate in a different way, to those facing firms in the more conventional sectors. It is for that reason that the volume emphasises the nature of the scientific labour market, the access to technology, the role of public procurement, and the importance of venture capital.

Although much attention has been paid to the problems facing those starting new enterprises there can be little doubt that it is the performance of the relatively few fast-growing small firms that can be important determinants of the growth of a local, regional or national economy. The present serious study addresses the barriers to growth which are faced by this group of firms.

David Storey
Small Business Centre,
University of Warwick

1

Barriers to Growth:
The ACARD Study

John Barber, Stanley Metcalfe, and Mike Porteous

Increasing attention has been paid in recent years to the important role played by small and medium-sized firms in innovation and economic growth. Special emphasis has been given in particular to the important stimulus small firms provide to competition in markets that might otherwise be dominated by large, established companies; their role in the early development and exploitation of radical new technologies (Rothwell and Zegveld 1982); and the job-creating effects of small firms (Storey 1982). The significance of all these effects, however, depends to a great extent on the ability of small firms, once established, to grow. While much attention has been given to the start-up of small enterprises, comparatively little is known about the ways in which small firms are able to realize their full innovative and growth potential, what the most important factors are which constrain their development and growth, or how these might be most effectively overcome. Innovative ability is, of course, an important source of growth, but as a firm seeks to move into new activities it will often come up against difficult choices and constraints which it perceives only imperfectly.

For this reason ACARD recognized the need for an original study aimed at examining the barriers to growth of small, innovative companies in the UK and drawing out any lessons for policy making and issues for future investigation. The main concern was to understand the barriers inhibiting the transition of small firms into medium- and large-sized companies, particularly those companies which show signs of innovative potential or which operate in high-technology areas. Small firms appear to face a number of difficulties in making this transition. Thus it was felt that attention should be concentrated on the ability of firms once established to grow; the process of start-up was looked upon as relevant only in so far as it imposed constraints on subsequent growth.

It was clear from the outset that the complexities of the growth process should not be underestimated nor should too much credence be given to apparently simple, single-minded solutions to the growth problem, e.g. a lack of finance. Growth implies much more than the ability to invest in best-practice facilities. It requires an ability to adapt and change, to be aware of markets and technological developments arising outside the firm, to make use of internal resources and to combine them effectively and continually with resources drawn from the environment. If these growth barriers are not overcome, then no matter how efficient the firm and how attractive its products it will remain of limited economic significance. More generally, the issue of growth barriers is one vital aspect of the ability of UK industry to keep pace with its international competitors.

As a first step it was decided to undertake a series of literature reviews of what is currently known about the most important factors influencing the growth of small firms in the UK. The aim was to identify gaps in the knowledge, the needs for further research, and the most appropriate lines of enquiry for any future investigation by ACARD. This book draws together the seven expert review papers prepared for the ACARD study, and represents the findings at this preliminary stage. Taken together these add up to a useful overview of the state of knowledge. A number of significant gaps emerged, however. As expected, rather more was known about the problems involved in starting new businesses than about the barriers to subsequent growth. The issues of finance, skills and management appeared to be the more researched, but even here little attention had been given to the more dynamic aspects of how these and other factors interact as the firm seeks to grow.

In this introduction we shall summarize the findings contained in the various papers, draw together the principal implications of these findings and suggest areas for future work. Before doing so we will help place the papers in their appropriate perspective by elaborating briefly on several of the general issues surrounding the role and growth of small firms.

SOME BACKGROUND ISSUES RELATING TO THE GROWTH OF FIRMS

This study is not primarily concerned with the factors encouraging the start-up of new companies or enterprises nor with the reason why many of them are likely to fail. Rather it is concerned with the growth and development of new firms and enterprises once successfully established. We take it for granted that a market economy needs to generate a large number of business experiments in a wide range of fields and that public policy should be concerned with whether the economic environment and the framework of incentives encourage this to take place.

Like other industrial economies, the UK is predominantly an economy of small firms with 83 per cent of all enterprises in 1985 having a turnover of less than £¼ million. This dominance is in part a reflection of the composition of the stock of enterprises. Roughly 65 per cent of all enterprises are in the services sector which is dominated by retailing and catering activities. Manufacturing, which is more prone to large-scale units, only amounts for 10 per cent of total enterprises. In the manufacturing sector itself, however, small enterprises also dominate. Statistics available from the 1984 census of production are summarized in Table 1.1.

Table 1.1: 1985 census of production statistics for small firms

Employees	No. of enterprises	% enterprises	% manufacturing gross output	% manufacturing employment
1–99	122,408	96.1	18.1	23.5
100–199	2,374	1.9	5.9	6.8
200–999	2,088	1.6	16.9	17.5
1,000 +	560	0.4	59.1	52.2
Total	127,430	100.0	100.0	100.0

The firms with more than 1,000 employees have, on average, 13 establishments per enterprise, while the firms in the smallest size class are typically single-establishment enterprises. It will be apparent from these figures that gross output per employee rises consistently with the size class of enterprise, being some 50 per cent greater in the largest enterprises than in the smallest. Of course, these aggregate statistics conceal considerable variations between individual manufacturing sectors.

Sectors within manufacturing which had the largest number of firms with less than 200 employees in 1985 were, in descending order: printing and publishing, which had nearly twice as many as any other sector; clothing, hats, and gloves; miscellaneous machinery and mechanical equipment; hand tools and finished metal goods; and wooden furniture and shop fittings. At the three-digit level of the Standard Industrial Classification (SIC) it is possible to identify 15 sectors for which in 1985 over half of the output was produced by small firms. Those with the highest proportion were, in descending order: miscellaneous wooden articles; miscellaneous manufacturing industries; metal working machine tools; saw-milling, planing, etc. of wood; bolts, nuts, and washers etc.; and builder's carpentry, and joinery. Not surprisingly many of the sectors in which small firms predominate tend to be drawn from the more traditional areas of manufacturing. However, 49 per cent of the output of measuring, checking and precision instruments was produced by small firms in 1985 while medical and surgical equipment (35 per cent of output accounted for by small firms), specialized chemical products industrial (33 per cent), and optical precision instruments (30 per cent) were among the more high-technology sectors in which small firms played a significant role.

Small firms appear to account for a very small proportion of R&D undertaken in the UK. (In 1978 firms with more than 1,000 employees appeared to account for 96 per cent of the total R&D undertaken by UK enterprises.) The available data almost certainly underestimate the share of R&D accounted for by small firms. Partly this is because of the coverage of the data which is necessarily much less complete for small than for large firms and partly because of the nature of technological activities in small firms, which typically do not have specialized and separately accountable R&D departments, relying instead on design and production engineering activities. According to figures produced by Pavitt (1987), R&D is the source of about 80 per cent of the knowledge inputs into innovations made by firms with more than 50,000 employees but only 40 per cent in the case of firms with between 100 and 499 employees compared to 49 per cent from design, production, and operating staff. Moreover while firms with less than 1,000 employees account for a very small proportion of total R&D, they accounted for nearly 40 per cent of significant innovations in the UK during the period 1975 to 1983. It is certain that R&D statistics give a very incomplete picture of the innovative capabilities of small companies.

As far as foreign trade is concerned small firms are much less likely to be involved in export markets than large firms. A recent study indicated that within manufacturing about 14 per cent of the firms with a turnover of less than £1m are exporters compared to about 48 per cent of firms with a turnover of between £1m and £10m, 63 per cent of firms with a turnover of between £10m and £100m, and 72 per cent of firms with a turnover of over £100m (Bannock and Partners 1987). An interesting feature of these figures is they appear to suggest that of those growing firms which make the difficult transition to become exporters a majority appear to do so while they are still relatively small.

The reasons why the size distribution of enterprises takes the particular shape that it does has been much debated but it need not long detain us here. Suffice it to say that the small-firms sector enjoys a considerable turnover, with 'births' of all enterprises averaging 12.5 per cent and 'deaths' of enterprises averaging 10.5 per cent in the first half of the 1980s, and that recent evidence indicates that the probability of survival increases with the size and the age of the enterprise (Evans 1987). The problem concerning ACARD was why so few firms made a successful transition out of the small size category. In some cases this will be because the natural economic size of a competitive unit is small, in others it will be because the firm sells to geographically limited, or otherwise specialized niche markets. However, in many cases such explanations of limited size are unsatisfactory. Neither diseconomies of scale nor niche markets need necessarily limit the size of the firm. Selling in the same niches overseas or developing products for new niches are both viable ways of overcoming limitations imposed by the size of particular domestic markets. Of course, there are many partial, and typically untested, hypotheses as to the real limitations on the growth of firms. Some emphasize external limitations, e.g. an unsympathetic banking community, failures of business education, or constricting government purchasing policies, while others put the emphasis on internal factors, such as the ability to change management structure at critical stages in the firm's growth (Grieve Smith and Fleck 1987) (Scott and Bruce 1987) or the, seemingly simple, unwillingness to increase beyond a certain size with all that may entail in terms of loss of independence and personal work relationships (Segal, Quince, and Partners 1985). What is clear is that we have little systematic understanding of which influences are important or how they might interact and bear upon different stages of the growth process.

An important related issue is the ability of the UK to exploit the commercial opportunities which new technology in the form of new products and processes will generate on a worldwide basis. In some sectors – for example, those producing specialized machinery – small firms tend to be the norm and enjoy important advantages. If the UK is to maintain an effective presence in these sectors the most important factors will be the ability to generate sufficient small firms which develop their specialist expertise in line with technological change and market needs. In these cases the success of firms will depend on adaptability, innovativeness, and successful qualitative change, while barriers to growth in size may have little relevance. Rather it is the capacity to transform the focus of the business at appropriate intervals which is crucial.

In many other sectors, however, while small firms may have an important role to play in the early stages of development of a new technology or product, market growth and the progress of technology soon shifts the balance of advantage to larger enterprises. Economies of scale in production, heavy upfront research and development costs, or the need for a global marketing network all require significance threshold investments which the smaller firm is not in a position to make. In some cases even firms which are large by UK standards may find it difficult to survive against foreign competition, particularly that emanating from US and Japanese firms, a factor which does much to explain the current interest in collaboration in both R&D and production. It is not altogether surprising to find (see p. 4) that R&D expenditures are concentrated in larger enterprises, as are UK exports.

The division between those technologies, products and markets in which small firms can play a major role and those in which large firms predominate is not a clear-cut one. Even in global markets dominated by giant multinationals, some smaller firms will be able to survive by exploiting particular market niches. There will indeed be many cases where this will be the most appropriate strategy for UK firms to follow and where an attempt to be a major producer would not be the best use of UK resources. Nevertheless, if the UK is unable to produce sufficient new businesses which can grow with, and maintain a significant share in, rapidly growing international markets in new products or processes, our ability to exploit the opportunities offered by new technology could be severely constrained and with it our ability to improve our standard of living.

Of course, only a small proportion of small firms can grow to be large or even medium-size firms by domestic, let alone international, standards. The important consideration is that conditions in the UK business environment should be sufficiently conducive to the growth and qualitative development of small firms, so that we can achieve an appropriate and effective presence in both domestic and international markets. What is meant by growth, whether it be measured by change in turnover, employment or capital assets, needs some brief comment. Here it is relevant to distinguish two basic patterns of economic growth. The first is through the addition of a series of new businesses, none of which typically grows beyond a relatively small size. The second entails growth in the size of one or more of a firm's existing businesses. The particular form which is appropriate, and indeed the appropriate mix between the two, will depend very much on the market and product involved. This mix will reflect, *inter alia*, the characteristics of the markets in which the firm operates, its technological resources, the pattern and pace of technological change and the nature and extent of various economies of scale and scope. It is the second type of growth pattern which is the primary concern of this study.

It will be obvious that, of itself, growth cannot be taken as a measure of performance without reference to the general growth of the market. It is often not difficult for a firm to achieve rapid absolute growth when the overall market is also expanding rapidly. In many situations a better index of competitive performance is growth relative to the market, that is, the change over time in a firm's market share. A firm which is expanding its market share is, by definition, more competitive than rivals with constant or falling market shares. Furthermore, because such a competitive firm is necessarily expanding its resource base relative to its rivals, it will be better placed to finance further capacity expansion, marketing efforts and technological innovation. In this way competitive success has a tendency to build upon competitive success. As a corollary, absolute growth can hide the fundamental long-term weakness of a firm's competitive position, a consideration which the recent ACARD reports on the software industry and medical equipment industry highlighted (ACARD 1986a). A failure to maintain a firm's relative market position undermines its long-term access to resources and may ultimately undermine its existence.

What is meant by the 'firm' in a particular market context also needs brief comment. It may mean an independent enterprise or it may mean a component part of a large multi-product, multi-divisional enterprise. In the latter case, the relations between the operating divisions and the parent firm will be an important influence upon the incentives and barriers to growth faced by each division. Businesses which are founded independently will face very different problems in attempting to grow from those faced by business units which are 'spun-off' within a large corporate organization. However, the growth prospect of all small firms, whether independent or not, will be affected by their relationship with larger firms whether the latter are cast in the role of customer, competitor, or suppliers of components, equipment, technology, or capital.

A small business unit embedded in a large firm may as it grows find it advantageous to obtain its independence through a management buy-out or to seek a change in corporate parent via sale and subsequent takeover. Conversely, for the independently founded business, its prospects for growth may be greatly enhanced through a strategic merger or takeover by a favourable corporate parent. All this emphasizes the importance of the market in complete businesses as well as illustrating the significance of the origins of businesses for explaining their subsequent growth. The willingness of large firms to acquire and develop smaller enterprises, while injecting necessary management skills, technology, and other resources on terms more favourable than could be obtained on the open market, would seem to be a quite crucial element in overcoming barriers to growth. None the less, some caution is needed here, for acquisition may also generate new barriers to growth if, for example, the additional activity is incompatible with the core businesses of the present company. These are vitally important organizational matters which require detailed attention.

In assessing the ability of small firms to grow, two further points must be borne in mind. First, that quantitative growth and qualitative change in the organization of the firm are inextricably linked; in general the former is only possible through the latter. Second, there is no clear-cut answer to the question, 'How small is a small firm?'. It depends upon the relevant technological and market environments and whether or not one takes an international or a domestic perspective. Consideration of the papers contained in this volume suggests that a flexible approach to the definition of firm size is required, and that rigid criteria, based on measures such as employment or turnover, can be very misleading.

THE LITERATURE REVIEWS

From the above considerations we have found it convenient to summarize the findings of the seven literature reviews under three headings: management and motivation, resources, and market opportunities and structure.

Management and motivation

A recurrent theme in a number of the papers, and one which reflects wider thinking on the problems of firms in general in the UK, is that of the attitudes and motivations of managers. It is sometimes said that British managers lack the entrepreneurial drive and abilities of many of their counterparts in other countries. The attitudes of UK managers towards technological change and innovation are taken to be a poor reflection of those in major competitor countries. It is also known that the qualifications and background of British managers compare very unfavourably. A related argument is that fewer top performers are attracted into careers in industry, partly because of the existence of a national culture which exhibits a long-standing bias against industry.

The first chapter, by Bosworth and Jacobs looks at the evidence on managerial attitudes and abilities. The paper is able to draw on a large number of empirical studies. These indicate that the occupational category of managers and administrators, the number of individuals in self-employment, and the size of the small-business sector all show rapid growth in recent years. The available studies, however, portray a consistent picture of lack of managerial training, relatively low qualifications and poor competence. The literature also points to several ways in which attitudes and motivations may restrict the expansion of small, owner-manager-run companies.

Here the evidence would seem to relate primarily to the very small owner-managed enterprise, of perhaps less than fifty employees. In this kind of firm, the owner-manager typically attempts to keep control of the key decision making and other important aspects of the business, resisting the pressure to delegate responsibilities. So long as the firm remains relatively small there may, of course, be some advantages to this unbureaucratic, informal style of management. Special conflicts are likely to be created, however, as soon as the firm faces opportunities

9

for expansion; the limits of managers' abilities to cope with all the different elements of the business quickly being reached. Contrary to widely held opinion, the problem may have little to do with any lack of entrepreneurial abilities on the part of owner-managers of small companies. Rather it is more that growth demands a different, more formal approach to management, involving delegation of responsibilities and decision making for the various functions of the business. Many owner-managers may prefer to opt for slower growth or sell out of the company than have control pass from their hands in this way.

A related aspect is that new management skills and competences are needed as the firm grows in size and a means must be developed of co-ordinating these effectively. In this context, the paper on market structure, by McGee, raises the possibility that lack of realistic planning and financial evaluation procedures will lead to systematic under-estimation of the costs of marketing and product development. The allocation of scarce resources – financial, technical or human – is a strategic issue which is often poorly understood by managers of small firms.

One must be careful not to place too much emphasis on the role of managerial attitudes in determining the performance of small firms as this can easily lead to the view that there is little the policy maker can do to remove barriers to growth. Entrepreneurial attitudes and motivation are in any case difficult to measure or assess in any precise way. However, attitudes to management and entrepreneurship are formed very much within wider social and educational conditions and policies can be formulated to create, for example, a more enterprise-driven culture. This brings us to the external determinants of small-firm growth with which the other papers are largely concerned.

Resources

The role which access to resources plays in determining the growth of small firms is the theme of the next three papers. These deal with three crucial resources: access to finance, skilled labour, and technology.

Access to finance has frequently been cited in the past as a key constraint on the growth of small firms in the UK and, more generally, on innovation. In his survey of capital market institutions, Hall deals with the long-standing issue of the alleged gap between the needs of small firms and the willingness of holders of capital to meet those needs. Clearly finance is a major resource, the lack of which can cripple growth prospects. This essay covers internal and external sources of finance, including various government-sponsored schemes, the unlisted securities market and corporate venturing. It is clear that not all the blame for capital market deficiencies can be placed upon the lenders. The owners and managers of small firms are often woefully lacking in their ability to present convincing business plans. Clearly there are great dangers here in treating finance as if it were a commodity divided into homogeneous bands of risk each carrying its own rate of interest. Finance is typically supplied in a package with potential lenders and borrowers often having quite different needs in terms of the elements of risk, security and repayment of principal implicit in the package. For companies basing their growth on the development of new technology, the potential for divergent assessment of risks, for example, is obviously considerable. Thus the question is not the availability of funds *per se* but availability at a price and conditions on which borrower and lender can agree.

The evidence covered in this survey makes it difficult to distinguish between the problems involved in starting a new firm and those which must relate to its subsequent survival and expansion. It is likely that different types of finance are required at different stages in the growth of small firms and for different kinds of expenditures, e.g. fixed investment, R&D, or working capital, but generally the literature appears to gloss over these distinctions. More specifically, the relation between finance for small firms and innovation has been largely ignored. For the purposes of defining a framework to analyse further these issues, it is the interaction between the internal capabilities of the firm and the way in which it combines its own resources with external sources of finance which offers the most fruitful direction for future enquiry.

Small firms are also likely to face special difficulties in attracting and retaining skilled labour. The evidence here, which Bosworth cites in his second paper, shows a consistent picture of wages and salaries per employee increasing with plant and firm size, suggesting that small firms tend to employ lower-qualified workers. There is also evidence of higher labour turnover in small firms. Lower levels of training – which in smaller firms tends to be more often of an informal rather than formal nature

11

– also appears to be associated with smaller size. Shortages of suitably skilled labour and low levels of training are, of course, very much part of a wider problem in the UK, yet it is clear that few studies have been able to assess the relationship between size of firm and access to and use of skilled labour.

A key issue which is raised in this paper is whether the decision to specialize in technologically more advanced areas by the growing firm leads to pressures on its deployment and development of skilled labour. As access to skilled labour is often crucial to the successful innovative performance of the firm, any evidence of small firms being specially disadvantaged in their capacity to train or recruit skilled labour has particular significance. The point made by Bosworth, however, is that there are two distinctive types of skilled labour shortage. One is the actual shortage that a firm may experience because of its current or planned activities. The second is a latent shortage because firms reconcile themselves to lower-level technology and slow growth, effectively avoiding the problems of overcoming actual shortages by default. Again though, as with the case of finance, the available literature often fails to make important analytical distinctions of this kind.

Perhaps the clearest answers to whether particular factors impose barriers to growth of small firms comes from the paper by Rothwell and Beesley on access to external technology. The paper draws on a relatively small number of studies in the literature but also on the considerable data base on innovations built up at the Science Policy Research Unit, on research in progress and on contacts with other experts in the area. Rothwell and Beesley (Chapter 5) argue that the findings show that access to external sources of technology is not a barrier to innovation and growth in small and medium firms. Where there is a problem it is more likely to be in the internal capability of small firms first to seek out and then to make use of the available sources of information and technologies. External technology is seen as a complement to, and not a substitute for, in-house technological efforts by innovative firms – the employment of qualified scientists and engineers being quite central to the technological development of the firm.

In this respect, the distinction between access to external sources of technical knowledge and information (such as from universities or through licensing agreements) and the internal technological expertise and resources of the firm is an important one. The samples of innovative firms which the paper largely draws upon are perhaps biased towards the finding that external technology is not a problem, and a sample of long-established small firms drawn from one of the more traditional sectors of industry might give a very different result. In any case too little is known about the problems faced by small firms in adapting and changing their internal technological resources as they grow, possibly seeking to enter more sophisticated or new areas of production or facing more technologically advanced demands.

The paper also raises an important issue for any research which was touched on briefly above. In attempting to identify the barriers to growth in small firms one must be careful not to argue that, because limitations exist to firms' access to resources (such as technology, skilled labour, trained management, or finance) these limitations are necessarily the binding constraints to the growth of small firms in the UK. Growth will also depend on the willingness and ability of small firms to exploit the availability of such resources to take advantages of the opportunities in the markets for their products. The explanation of the growth of small firms lies in the interaction between the inherent motivation and capabilities of the firms themselves and the external environment in which they must endeavour to survive and prosper.

Market opportunities and structures

The success of small firms will be significantly influenced by the market structures within which they operate and the opportunities which these markets present. The characteristics of demand in particular markets represent one set of important influences including market growth, the size and frequency of purchases, the degree of market segmentation, and the possibility of creating niches which small firms can exploit. Another set of factors relates to the strategies followed by large firms and the opportunities available to small firms either to collaborate with other firms in a variety of ways or even to merge. This is an area in which there is a relative paucity of empirical evidence and research. For this reason the three papers included under this heading tend either to rely on *a priori* reasoning or to draw tentative inferences from research in related areas or from the few empirical studies that have been carried out.

The first of these papers by Hartley and Hutton looks at the impact on small firms of the purchasing policy of large organizations both in the private and public sectors. The opportunities for growth and innovation enjoyed by small firms are determined to a considerable extent by the propensity of large firms and organizations to procure goods and services from outside suppliers and the manner in which this is done.

Hartley and Hutton argue that large organizations can derive considerable benefits by purchasing from small firms – such as lower cost, greater speed and flexibility of response, and more innovative products. However, the information costs involved in seeking out small suppliers and the perceived risk that products purchased from unknown suppliers may be unsatisfactory, together with the incentive structure facing employees in large organizations, may mean that much of this potential is not realized. For their part, small firms may be unwilling or unable to incur the information costs of seeking out opportunities for selling to large complex organizations. Moreover, as McGee points out, the small firm placed between large buyers and large suppliers may find its growth limited by their exercise of market power, particularly when that small firm lacks distinctive competitive advantage.

The costs and difficulties of small firms wishing to sell to large purchasers may be greatly affected by the procurement practices of the latter. Centralized purchasing, which tends to be risk-averse in choosing suppliers, prone to using costly and complex tendering procedures, conservative in specifying requirements, and generally slow, does not appear to favour the chances of small firms. Decentralized procurement policies, which involve more and smaller contracts, make it easier for small suppliers to gain a foothold. On the other hand, once a small firm does make its way on to the list of approved suppliers, centralized procedures make it easier for the firm to expand its sales and grow, particularly if it can benefit from economies of large-scale production.

The second paper by Hughes examines the impact of merger activity, restrictive trade practices, and competition policy on the growth prospects of small firms and on their capacity to innovate. Mergers and collaborative agreements with other firms may in certain circumstances provide small firms with an alternative strategy for growth and development and a means to gain access to capital, management, markets, specialist skills, and technology. They may also enable small firms to enjoy economies of scale and scope in activities such as R&D and to achieve lower costs by rationalization of, for example, product ranges and marketing arrangements. At the same time merger activities and anti-competitive behaviour by large companies may inhibit the growth and development of small firms. However, where small companies are not quoted and/or are closely held the likelihood of a takeover against the wishes of owner-management is remote. In any case the possibility of selling out may be an important element in the incentive to develop a business.

The ability of small firms to merge and enter into relationships with larger companies may have a significant role to play in the innovation process. Although small firms may sometimes have an advantage in the initial phase of development of a new product or process, subsequent development may be most effectively undertaken by acquisition or integration of the smaller organization within a larger firm. However, the greater flexibility and more informal corporate style which is the source of much successful innovation by small firms may not survive within the confines of a larger organization. The recent increase in the number of management buy-outs may be a reflection of the difficulties faced by small businesses trying to operate as part of large organizations.

The impact of mergers and inter-firm collaboration on the growth prospects of small firms will vary with the circumstances of each case. Hughes finds that there has been very little systematic research either of the relative merits of mergers and collaborative agreements as strategies for small firms and that there is little hard evidence of the impact of these activities on small-firm performance.

The final paper by McGee brings together a number of issues in the context of the appropriate strategic stance of small, growing firms. Sustaining the growth of a firm depends upon the continuous development of product and cost advantages but often at the cost of straining the innovative and marketing resources of the firm. The challenge facing the growing firm can become particularly acute as markets and technological advantages are progressively refined. Small firms typically begin as simple businesses but sustained growth requires a transition to business complexity in which a firm expands its skill base, explores new market and product opportunities, and develops an appropriate managerial structure. The challenge facing the growing firm can be stated in terms of a move from relatively narrow market niches in which it exploits a narrow range of distinctive assets into a situation in which it serves a larger number of market segments with a much broader skills and knowledge base. As McGee points out, the early growth of the firm often hides longer-term strategic weaknesses, with the growth of the firm reflecting the general growth of its market rather than any distinctive advantages. Not all small firms will be able to transcend their origins, but those that do are likely to have a clear idea of the true costs of marketing and product development and to understand the principles of strategic resource allocation. In short, McGee concludes that the fundamental barriers to growth are internal to the firm, that is, they are managerial in nature.

This conclusion, however, reflects the approach adopted in the paper whilst none the less pointing to real difficulties of achieving growth (further outlined in the next section). McGee's conclusion therefore is perhaps best taken more as a working hypothesis that may be useful for structuring research on firms each operating in their specific market conditions. It is the interaction of the evolving internal resources of the firm and changes in its environment and opportunities for growth which are likely to offer the most fruitful lines of enquiry.

THE PROCESS OF GROWTH IN SMALL FIRMS

Looking forward

Now that we have outlined the main themes contained in the reviews, it will help at this stage if we present a statement of what they suggest about the growth process in small firms. If a firm is to establish itself successfully on a path of sustained expansion it must obviously satisfy a number of requirements for growth. It must expand its sales, it must have access to additional resource inputs, it must expand its management team and it must expand its technological and market knowledge base. Each of these growth requirements involves a different set of problems for the management of the firm to solve and the possible solutions to these problems give rise to a variety of growth strategies and alternative development paths for the firm. Sales growth may simply come with the general growth of the markets for its existing products, with greater difficulty it will come as the firm expands the market share of its existing product range at the expense of its rivals. Even more difficult to achieve is the sales growth which

16

comes from the extension of the product range, perhaps involving innovations which take the firm into entirely new markets (Rothwell and Zegveld 1982). Growth of the firm will generally require it to expand some, if not all, of the elements in its labour force, to acquire additional working and fixed capital resources, and to ensure that its supply of material and semi-finished inputs expands appropriately. The latter may involve the firm in detailed negotiations with suppliers, while additional capital resources may involve access to the banking system and the capital markets. Expanding the labour force may, in turn, require the firm to set up its own internal training and skill-enhancement programmes.

Some of the most difficult problems facing the growing firm will relate to its management needs. The monitoring, co-ordination, and control of the activities in a growing firm will require the utilization of increasing amounts of information, placing an increasing burden on management. Communication systems within the firm become of crucial importance and impose qualitative change on the management style of the firm as informal systems based on daily personal contact are replaced by structured, formal control systems which extend the impersonal exchange of information (Connell 1985). With growth, the founding entrepreneurs must ultimately be willing to relinquish many day-to-day control functions and delegate these tasks to an enlarged, specialized management team. It is clear that one of the secrets of successful growth is not only to recognize and capitalize upon external opportunities but also to recognize and implement appropriate changes in the firm's internal organization. A failure to make these changes will often lead to an erosion of profitability and will ultimately call into question the firm's very survival.

In expanding its knowledge base, the firm can rely on internal mechanisms such as R&D or design activities but typically it must match them with external sources of knowledge. Close interaction with customers and suppliers, links with higher education and other public-sector research institutions, and collaborate ventures with other firms can all provide means of acquiring technological and commercial information. This involves the difficult problems of scanning the world outside the firm and of transferring externally generated knowledge into the firm in an effective way.

Under each of these headings barriers to the expansion of the firm will arise with their incidence changing over time as markets and technology themselves change. Some of these barriers will be external to the firm, that is, they are properties of the firm's operating environment which it cannot change. No doubt the classic example of this is the risk aversion which banks and capital markets are alleged to show in the face of investment opportunities in small, new-technology enterprises. But many of the barriers will be internal, generated within the firm by its very growth. Typically these will arise at particular crisis points when the firm must cross a significant threshold, e.g. a major shift in its make or buy policy for components or the need to set up a separate marketing department. It is of great interest to know how the various internal and external barriers interact along the growth path of the firm. Unfortunately, in the present state of knowledge, our reviewers had to treat their topics in isolation and the remedying of this deficiency will be a major problem for future research.

So far we have looked at the growth process in terms of opportunities and resource needs. Equal attention has to be given to incentives. For there is no automatic requirement even in the most benign of circumstances, that a firm will grow. Growth requires a conscious commitment by the strategic decision makers of the firm and therefore a propensity to foresee benefits from growth commensurate with the costs of growth. Attitudes to material wealth and the fiscal system are important here but it would be a crude error to imagine that the pecuniary stimulus to growth is the sole, dominant one. In some cases the aim is to found a business empire, with profits being the means rather than the end. In other cases growth is deliberately avoided for fear that the independence of the founding entrepreneurs may be lost. Only if the founders can be encouraged to sell their enterprise will this barrier be overcome. Clearly, the taxation of income and capital is not an irrelevant consideration when incentives to growth are being considered.

In focusing attention on the interaction between growth barriers at different stages in the life of the firm and the way in which the incidence of different barriers changes over time, this study suggests a rich agenda for future research. It would be particularly interesting to compare the growth performance of different firms operating in both similar and different technological and market environments to identify causes of 'fast' and 'slow' growth. Further study of the international factors affecting the growth of small firms, the role of corporate venturing, and informal and formal links between large and small firms would certainly be of value in understanding barriers to growth.

On the policy front it is not possible to draw definitive conclusions at this stage. But, in general terms, it might suggest that enterprise policy has two main concerns: increasing the net birth rate of firms and running more enterprise experiments; and creating an environment in which a sufficient number of these enterprises grow to significance on both a domestic and international scale. Governments typically employ a wide range of policies to stimulate the small-firm sector (Cross 1983). How they influence growth barriers and how they interact in an offsetting or reinforcing way is less clear. Too piecemeal an approach to the different aspects of enterprise policy is obviously undesirable.

REFERENCES

ACARD (1986a) *Medical Equipment*, London: HMSO.

ACARD (1986b) *Software: A Vital Key to Competitiveness*, London: HMSO.

Bannock, Graham and Partners (1987) *Into Active Exporting*, London: British Overseas Trade Board.

Connell, D. (1985) *The Management of Growth in High Technology Companies*, London: Deloitte, Haskins, and Sells.

Cross, M. (1983) 'The United Kingdom', in Storey, D.J. (ed.), *The Small Firm*, Beckenham: Croom Helm.

Evans, D.S. (1987) 'Tests of alternative theories of firm growth', *Journal of Political Economy*, 95.

Grieve Smith, J. and Fleck, V. (1987) 'Business strategies in small high-technology companies', *Long Range Planning*, 20.

Pavitt, K. (1987) 'The size of structure of British technological activities', *Scientometrics*, 1987.

Rothwell, R. and Zegveld, W. (1982) *Innovation and the Small and Medium Sized Firm*, London: Frances Pinter.

Scott, M. and Bruce, R. (1987) 'Five stages of growth in small businesses', *Long Range Planning*, 20.

Segal, Quince, and Partners (1985) *The Cambridge Phenomenon: The Growth of High Technology in a University Town*, Cambridge: Segal, Quince, and Partners.

Storey, D.J. (1982) *Entrepreneurship and the Small Firm*, Kent: Croom Helm.

2

Management Attitudes, Behaviour, and Abilities as Barriers to Growth

Derek Bosworth and Chris Jacobs

GROWTH OF MANAGEMENT AND SELF-EMPLOYMENT

The occupational category of managers and administrators grew steadily from 1971 to 1981, at around 2.4 per cent per annum (IER 1986, p. 6). While the period 1971 to 1986 was one of more moderate growth, the occupation is forecast to grow at nearly 1.8 per cent per annum to 1990. Growth rates for this group are higher than the average for all occupations and their forecast share of employment rises from 2.4 per cent in 1971 to 3.5 per cent in 1990. While the share of self-employment was fairly stable over the long term between 1950 and 1980 (falling slightly from 8.6 to 8.0 per cent), it increased significantly in the early 1980s (reaching 11 per cent by 1985) (Wilson and Bosworth 1986). The growth in self-employment corresponds with the growth in the small-business sector which, after the secular decline from 1930 to 1970, has grown significantly (Storey 1982; Cross 1983; Wilson and Bosworth 1986, pp. 19–21). Self-employment is expected to continue growing over the period 1984 to 1990 by over 300,000, compared with a decline of almost 200,000 of employees in employment (Wilson and Bosworth 1986, p. 21; IMS/OSG 1986). While there is a marked lack of information about the number of female owner-managers (and even less about ethnic minorities), a recent estimate put female owner-managers at 6 per cent of the small-business sector (Clutterbuck and Devine 1985), and an even smaller proportion of owner-managers employing over 25 employees (Wilson and Bosworth 1986).

BACKGROUND OF SMALL-BUSINESS OWNER-MANAGERS

There are a number of similarities between UK and US managers, but important differences with our continental competitors (Swords-Isherwood 1980). Similarities between UK and Australian management have also emerged (Pym 1971) at a time when an unflattering picture of Australian management is being painted (England 1975; Byrt and Masters 1974; Blandy *et al.* 1985). UK management does not appear to be a coherent elite, nor a highly educated, technically competent group; mobility from the shop floor is attributed more to the low status of the occupation than to efficiency of this recruitment pattern (Swords-Isherwood 1980). Business and finance undergraduates had the highest *ex ante* rates of return to higher education of any group at one university (Bosworth and Ford 1985) and *ex post* rates of return to entering business professions have been above the average for all professions in recent years (Wilson 1984). However, improvements in the quality of UK management are slow (Swords-Isherwood 1980), and likely to be even slower among small firms (without the resources or ability to supplement the education and training of potential future managers or to hire and effectively absorb new, qualified talent from the external pool). There appears a considerable amount that can be learnt from other countries (Ford 1983), particularly the West German emphasis on training and the Japanese experiments with the social organization of the firm, outlined below.

Despite a growing number of female entrepreneurs, most small-business owner-managers are male, married and middle-aged (Ritchie *et al.* 1982). A proportion claims some form of higher education, but the general view appears to be that there is an identifiable lack of basic education amongst UK small-business owner-managers (Ritchie *et al.* 1982; Gill 1985). While some owner-managers have prior experience of running a business, or have worked in a managerial capacity for larger companies, the majority have received no formal management training.

Small-business owner-managers also tend to be geographically immobile (Ritchie *et al.* 1982). It is difficult to generalize, but the owner-managers' lifestyles divide into two groups: lower middle-class owners and upper middle-class owners. The former tend to have a comfortable but unspectacular lifestyle, with fairly low monetary payments from the business masking a good standard of living due to the self-allocation of fringe benefits; the latter

21

pursue a more entrepreneurial lifestyle, with, on balance, a higher standard of living. Evidence suggests that small-business owner-managers experience major problems when taking the decision to expand and when faced by an expanding business. In most instances, the problems arise as a result of a mixture of personal, attitudinal, and management inadequacies (although some studies play down the latter: Boswell 1973). Many owner-managers are aware of their limitations in terms of management skills, particularly in the area of financial forward planning (Scase and Goffee 1980; Boswell 1973).

Case study evidence suggests that female entrepreneurs tend on average to be either significantly younger or older than their male counterparts (Watkins and Watkins 1986), following the normal life-cycle pattern of participation in the labour market. Females face specific educational barriers in both business start-up and growth (Watkins and Watkins 1986). However, those that progress through to higher education in business subjects appear to have broadly the same *ex ante* rate of return as their male counterparts (Bosworth and Ford 1985), although this partly arises because the lost income from alternative employment is lower. It has been argued that female owner-managers also face considerable career discrimination, particularly in finance and accounting (Clutterbuck and Devine 1985). The result is that the female entrepreneur tends to be less experienced, both managerially and technically, than her male counterpart. UK female owner-managers are still disadvantaged *vis-à-vis* their US counterparts, with regard to the prevailing social and economic cultures of the two countries (Clutterbuck and Devine 1985).

PERSONAL AND SOCIAL COSTS OF GROWTH

There are heavy personal and social costs in both the start-up and growth phases of a business, for entrepreneurs and their families. The entrepreneur's family has no reliable income parameters on which to base consumption decisions. Some entrepreneurs become disenchanted when current material success fails to compensate for the personal costs incurred (Scase and Goffee 1980). The entrepreneurial spouse, often the wife, makes important sacrifices to the business (i.e. space, labour time, and support). The business and the home tend to become intertwined, financially and in the use of the home for business purposes. Time is in short supply, and the wife and family are often denied the company and the time and attention of the entrepreneur. The wife finds herself bearing a triple burden (worker, housekeeper, and chief child-rearer) with little support from her husband. These factors strain family relationships (Scase and Goffee 1980). As growth takes place the strains increase, although a clearer distinction tends to develop between family and business, and the role of the wife tends to change from administrator to image promoter. The relationship between the owner-manager and the spouse and the spouse's attitudes are therefore crucial to growth (Gill 1985). In addition, the absence of inheritor children, the lack of a competent successor, the involvement of too many family members, and family conflict can all reduce the motivation for growth. Many owner-managers prefer to forego growth because of the associated high personal and family costs.

ENTREPRENEURIAL ATTITUDES AND MOTIVATION

Entrepreneurial attitudes mould the goals of the enterprise. Traditional theories view the small firm as owner-managed and profit maximizing for at least two reasons: net revenues (profits) form the owner-manager's income and they are assumed to be located in competitive areas where profit maximization is necessary for survival (Wildsmith 1973). Alternative, managerial theories of the firm view the larger firm as oligopolistic, where ownership and control are divorced (Koutsoyiannis 1975). Theories of managerial discretion suggest that management behaviour is not only a function of salary, but also of security, status, power, prestige, social service and professional excellence (Wildsmith 1973, pp. 68–9). Operationalization of this in the Williamson (1967a) model distinguishes salary, staff and emoluments in the managerial utility function. Clearly, under these assumptions, the owner-managed firm will remain smaller than the managerial, utility maximizing firm. Certain elements of these alternative models may be relevant to the behaviour of smaller firms (i.e. for tax reasons, emoluments may appear separately in the owner-manager's utility function), but it is primarily the difference in staffing in the Williamson (1967a) model that causes differences in internally generated growth and size.

In practice, while the acquisition of material reward is a significant motivation for business ownership, it is seldom prioritized by small-business owners (Gill 1985). They tend to emphasize job satisfaction and personal fulfilment (Ritchie *et al.* 1982; Clutterbuck and Devine 1985), much of which devolves from close contact with the business client group. An artisan philosophy, centred around the values placed on client satisfaction and the quality of the service or product (Gill 1985), linked with the avoidance of bureaucracy, has often inhibited the motivation for growth (Stanworth and Curran 1986; Scase and Goffee 1980).

This stylized view should be modified somewhat to account for two categories of owner-manager: the 'artisan' and the 'entrepreneurial', with different attitudes towards growth (Stanworth and Curran 1986). While ownership itself, and the status that this infers, may be more important than salary (Clutterbuck and Devine 1985; Ritchie *et al.* 1982), the distinction between material reward and ownership is not clear-cut because the economic value of ownership is equal to the discounted sum of future earnings (including the end-of-period capital value), and these depend on continued ownership. Nevertheless, ownership appears to confer more than just a stream of future income flows on the owner-manager. Male owner-managers exhibit both a drive for independence and a desire to control their life and working environment (Ritchie *et al.* 1982; Clutterbuck and Devine 1985; Gill 1985). Desire for control includes the control of others, and this can determine the direction and extent of the growth of the small business. However, the individual's dislike of bureaucratic processes (a major motive for small business start-ups) may also be a barrier to growth (Gill 1985; Stanworth and Curran 1986). 'Control loss', associated with the transmission of information accurately through successive layers of administration (Williamson 1967b), reflects the failure of the management and organizational structure to cope with conditions of too-rapid growth or, at any given point in time, too large a size. The owner-manager may fear the increased difficulty of ensuring that his decisions are put into effect as the layers of management increase (Sawyer 1981, p. 55).

While females share the male desire to control and the need for independence, they experience an added frustration with the male-dominated business-world ethos, which, to them, forms an 'accepted' philosophy, denying equal opportunities in terms of experience, recognition and promotion (Clutterbuck and Devine 1985). Pilot survey evidence suggests that a larger percentage of UK female owner-managers adopt a parental (maternal) role model, which focuses on creativity and team work, rather than on a style based on authoritarian control (Watkins and Watkins 1986).

UK small-business owner-managers tend to lie on the right of the political spectrum which, when linked with their desire to maintain control of their business, affects attitudes to trade unions and, thereby, to growth, as unionization (Bain and Elias 1985) and perhaps also union activity, increases with firm size (Sawyer 1981, p. 55). Empirical evidence does point to a positive trade union wage mark-up (Stewart 1983; Blanchflower 1983), even if it is smaller than once supposed (Minford 1983). Attitudes may differ in other countries, as in the Communist- and Socialist-based small firms of the Emilia Romagna region of Italy.[1] Here the common politics of the workers and owners give rise to interesting differences and quite different problems in the bargaining process. In the Emilia Romagna case, although union membership is lower in smaller than larger businesses, at around 20 per cent it is still high.

The managerial model of firm growth, for example, suggests that the valuation ratio of a company initially rises with growth and then declines (Marris 1964; Wildsmith 1973, pp. 92–8, 113–122). Continued ownership and control depend on avoiding under- and over-performance of the firm which might result in liquidation or takeover. While this is true of both types of manager, growth figures more heavily in the utility function of the professional manager than the owner-manager, other things equal, leading to a higher rate of profit and lower growth rate for the owner-managed firm. Given their views about control, owner-managers might be wary of growth that makes flotation of the company necessary. While a surprising proportion of the largest UK and US companies are still owner-controlled (Burch 1972; Chevalier 1969; Nyman and Silberston 1978; Sawyer 1981, pp. 161–3), the extent of owner-control decreases with size. However, both owner-control and managerial discretion have declined with the growth in institutional shareholdings (Stanworth and Giddens 1975; Sawyer 1981, pp. 163–5). While our focus is on privately owned firms, the argument is still important because small businesses not only see the loss of control in large companies, but also associate more rapid expansion with the use of external funds, which may be expensive and imply some loss of control to the funding institution. Such views are reinforced by the stigma attached to bankruptcy in the UK compared with the

USA, making the owner-manager reluctant to force the valuation ratio down too far, and manifesting itself in the form of practical difficulties in financing future ventures. Social attitudes to failure influence the risk aversion of entrepreneurs.

GROWTH AND THE MARKET

Small-business owners regard the market as one of their major difficulties, the area of management where they exert greatest effort and a major influence on the firm's potential for growth (Scase and Goffee 1980). Management planning and evaluation skills are scarce in the average small business, and long-term planning allied to company goals is rare. There are several responses to such problems, for instance: membership of trade associations and chambers of commerce, etc., which can provide access to expertise and the like (i.e. as in the case of the National Conference of Artisans in the Emilia Romagna region); greater provision of management training and advice related to business plans (Boswell 1973). Their problems revolve around: competition with established, often larger companies; existence of superior or lower-priced products; delivery dates; the need to upgrade services; devising strategies to circumvent shortages of demand (Storey 1985). While small-business owners in the UK generally hold a free-market philosophy, in practice they also try to insulate themselves from the fluctuations of the market (i.e. the creation of a personal service, diversification, and/or large company contract arrangements). However, this is equally true of Socialist- and Communist-based small firms in the Emilia Romagna region of Italy. Protection from the market during difficult times can aid small-business growth.

GROWTH AND THE LABOUR MARKET

Owner-managers worry about generating sufficient product demand to ensure that workers are fully employed and can be paid. These problems increase as the firm grows because of limits on the capacity to supervise the quality of the product (Scase and Goffee 1980). The owner-manager's insistence on personal contact and control makes delegation of decisions unattractive (Boswell 1973). Owner-managers report difficulties in hiring

26

competent, specialist staff willing to shoulder 'real responsibility' for decision making (Scase and Goffee 1980). On the other hand, on balance, small firms tend to select low-cost/low-quality options and, at the wage levels they pay, it is difficult to attract staff with such decision-making skills (Bosworth 1987). Despite awareness of their own managerial inadequacies, several studies report an unwillingness to recruit specialist staff or to use management consultants (Boswell 1973; Gill 1985). Some owner-managers see an enlarged workforce (particularly where the individuals are more experienced or qualified) as a threat to their personal control and prestige; the more so, the less able is the owner-manager. It is the professional, often highly qualified workers who are more closely associated with higher productivity and faster growth (Melman 1951; Fleming 1970). These factors are fuelled by fears of losing a 'trust' relationship with the workforce and the exposure of personal and management deficiencies in the owner. They are also influenced by the fact that the larger concern may have to cope with trade unions and employment legislation, which are viewed as an intrusion into personal autonomy by the average small-business owner (Scase and Goffee 1980). Small-business owners assert that informal and flexible personal relationships work best, and that egalitarian principles of staff management need to be viewed with caution. Equally, unions tend to view non-unionized small firms as 'sweatshops' (Rainnie and Scott 1986). Opinions about the effects of employment legislation also tend to polarize (Westrip 1986).

TECHNOLOGICAL CHANGE

Conservative attitudes and the independence ethos of owner-managers can hinder the introduction of change. Scarcity of time and expertise impinge on essential planning and staff retraining requirements. There is a reluctance to use information retrieval systems, and this results in inadequate knowledge of progress in the business or developments in the market. Small-business owners lack the evaluation skills necessary for costing techno-logical change. 'Hidden' costs can be overlooked and, subse-quently, prove difficult to absorb. Fear of new systems stems, in part, from an inadequate knowledge of complex new technology, and this hinders investment decisions. In addition, traditional, conservative attitudes towards external financing, along with an inability of owner-managers to cope effectively with financial management, link with real limitations on the general availability of low-cost finance for small businesses to hinder the adoption of expensive new technologies.

It has been realized for some time that the type and level of technology tends not only to vary with the size of the firm, but also to have implications for the organization of the firm (Veblen 1906; Woodward 1966). Smaller firms tend to operate with one-off (i.e. unit) and small-batch processes, and their level of technology is, on average, lower than larger firms. By implication, the introduction of new technologies often involves reorganization of the administrative structure (Woodward 1966). In essence, higher levels of technology involve more formal management structures with longer lines of command and a greater proportion of more highly qualified employees within the workforce (Woodward 1966, p. 51). In so far as technological development tends to lead the firm from unit production through batch (of various sizes) to process, there is a tendency for things to get worse before they get better *vis-à-vis* the types of problems which figure as important amongst owner-managers (Woodward 1966, pp. 65–7). The link between organization and technology provides another potential barrier for the small-firm owner-manager: it implies more major changes than supposed; it raises the question of the competence of the owner-manager to steer these changes through; it may be inconsistent with the owner-manager's attitudes to loss of control, bureaucracy, etc.; the process of development is stressful (both for the owner-manager and the organization) and fraught with dangers.

MANAGEMENT, ORGANIZATION, AND GROWTH

Small businessmen tend to view management as 'self-management', concerned with their own use of time, rather than the management of all of the firm's resources (Boswell 1973, p. 70). As the firm grows, there has to be a shift of attention away from the owner to the factor employed within the firm. Managerial and organizational change depends on the way in which the firm grows. This is not just a matter of the choice of technology, as evidence accumulates that a given technology can often be used in a variety of ways and, thus, management choices become important. The types of growth outlined in the organizational psychology literature (Katz and Kahn 1966) are:

(i) Growth by unit size (adding one or two more staff within an existing administrative unit)
(ii) Growth by parallel units (the multiplication of parallel units, i.e. opening another largely identical branch)
(iii) Growth by differentiation
(iv) Growth by specialization (entailing the redesign and reallocation of work functions)
(v) Growth by merger and takeover

On average, the extent of organizational change increases from the first to the second type of growth outlined above, and can be expected to be most marked in the final three categories (Anderson and Warkov 1961; Pondy 1969; Thompson 1967). Turning the argument around, if the owner-manager is unwilling to relax control of the firm, growth will be limited to certain types (i.e. the first two), and this may limit the potential for growth. This argument arises again in the context of the firm as a social system (see page 31, 'Alternative areas and forms of growth'), where we add a further category: growth by multi-skilling, participation and autonomous workgroups. The traditional concept of 'internal' (as opposed to 'external') growth implies that firms wishing to grow faster than their rivals must introduce better-designed products and more efficient productive systems than their rivals, which establishes a virtuous circle of profits and growth (Nelson and Winter 1974; Nelson et al. 1974). This leads us back to the theme discussed on page 27 under 'Technological change'.

Small-business owner-managers tend to prefer 'informal' communication and control structures which, in reality, allow for tight owner-control and which, in practice, may be needed for flexible adaptation to changing staffing requirements or market fluctuations. Growth involves a movement away from informal management structures towards more formal systems. As the organization grows, there is a need for new channels of communication and a controlled interaction of subsystems. In general, the typical owner-manager may resist such changes, as he tends to view them as alienating and bureaucratic, threatening personal control and prestige. The managerial and behavioural models of the firm paint a picture which suggests that these fears may be well founded (Williamson 1964, 1967a; Pondy 1969; Cyert and March 1963). While the extent of managerial slack can be policed, there are clearly costs of doing so, and some slack remains even if policing is expanded to the point where marginal costs equal marginal benefits. Empirical evidence tends to support the existence of other, non-profit managerial objectives amongst non-owner-controlled firms (Steer and Cable 1977).

In moving from small to large size, however, the firm chooses between different forms of internal organization and, by implication, between different types and intensities of control. The stylized view of the development of the firm has modified over time. The original view was that growth meant a switch from a profit-orientated goal structure (i.e. of the owner-manager) to a situation where the (non-profit) goals of the professional manager were given more weight. The current view is that there is a further stage in corporate development that switches the goal structure back, giving a higher weighting to profits. Williamson and Bhargava (1972), for example, suggest three main categories of firm:

(i) Traditional, unitary (U-form)
(ii) Divisionalized holding companies, without internal control apparatus (H-form)
(iii) Multi-divisionals, with separation of operational and strategic decision making, incorporating internal control apparatus (M-form)

While the developments are linked with firm size (Steer and Cable 1977), it is not entirely clear at what stages these transitions are successfully achieved, neither is the probability of maintaining owner-manager control (although, as argued earlier, the extent of such control would be lower even if the owner-manager existed in the M-form, assuming the owner-manager survived the transitional H- and M-form phases).

Certainly, the balance of evidence suggests that large, owner-controlled firms out-perform manager-controlled firms in terms of both profitability and growth (Radice 1971; Steer and Cable 1977). However, as we noted on page 26, owner-managers may be unwilling to dilute their personal power and control over the organization by adding professional, non-family personnel, even if it means accepting a lower profit (Pondy 1969). This occurs even though there are examples where the owner has been financially enormously better off, even with complete loss of control over the business (Brooks 1971, pp. 152–84). The current literature still views management attitudes as a major determinant (see page 23), but they may not be the only factor at play. The studies of organizational performances have noted that the large, high-performance owner-controlled firms may be atypical in having 'exceptionally efficient' management (Radice 1971; Steer and Cable 1977, p. 14). Thus, the perceived net benefits amongst the remainder of the owner-manager stock may be much lower. Perceived returns to growth will also be affected by the age of the owner-manager concerned. Little is known about the social and economic consequences for small-business owner-managers who attempt to grow, but, in doing so, lose control (as opposed to those who go bankrupt).

ALTERNATIVE AREAS AND FORMS OF GROWTH

The politics of small business has invariably accepted the 'corporate ageism' philosophy. Little research has sought to challenge these assumptions which began with Marshall, extended through Schumpeter and the Bolton Committee. They are still reflected in current policy and research, which concentrates on 'infant birth and mortality', neglecting the continued stagnation and failure of older small businesses. The prevailing ethos is that innovation is primarily linked to the new and the young business. We still work on the assumption that aging managements, linked with conservative attitudes, inhibit the growth of owner-managed small businesses. New small firms have been able to take advantage of preferential subsidies. By implication, the older small business continues to face discrimination with little evidence to back up ideological over-generalizations (Richie 1986).

Different environments in other countries indicate the possibility of quite distinct forms of organizational development. The experience of the Emilia Romagna region of Italy provides an example of business growth without company growth.[2] Artisan companies are restricted in size and there are strong financial inducements to remain small, because of the availability of low-cost finance for small businesses. However, this limitation on size does not appear to have restricted the technological dynamism or the export performance of these firms. Growth takes place by the development of new small enterprises with an existing owner-manager in the role of partner in the new concern. The analogies here with interlocking directorships are complicated by the fact

31

that most of the literature in this area deals with the hidden monopoly power of large companies (Dooley 1969; Johnson and Apps 1979; Kotz 1979; Sawyer 1981).

There is also a current upsurge of interest in the concept of the firm as a social organization, stimulated in part by the performance of Japan (Blandy et al. 1985). This has moved the productivity and growth debate one step further away from the over-simplistic arguments of technological determinism found in Taylorism. Recent work has argued that the result of Taylorism has been a poor quality of working life, low morale, low productivity and persistent industrial conflict (Emery and Phillips 1976; Lansbury and Spillane 1983; Hackman and Oldham 1980; Kriegler 1980; Blandy et al. 1985). The result is a trend away from traditional and towards 'more participative and flexible' management structures (Blandy et al. 1985, p. 72). It has been argued that the nature of the interaction between workers, management and the organization may be a more important influence on productivity and growth than technological change per se (Bosworth and Dawkins 1983, pp. 208–11), or the choice of formal organizational structure or the financial incentives offered to employees (Nelson 1981). The aim is to bring worker and company goals into line through worker participation in decision making and redesigning tasks to incorporate a wider range of activities, giving the worker greater autonomy and a broader appreciation of the overall production operations (Blandy et al. 1985, pp. 61–90). This development involves small operating units (Peters and Waterman 1983), and while, for this reason, it may appear particularly relevant to the small business, its ethos may seem to be alien to most UK owner-managers.

MANAGERIAL ABILITIES AND TRAINING

The capacity of the top controller (Sawyer 1981, p. 55) or management team (Penrose 1959) forms the ultimate limit to the rate of sustainable growth. The low quality of small-business owner-managers has been a major theme of this chapter (consistent with the evidence presented in Bosworth 1987), for example, in basic managerial skills and in the areas of finance and long-term planning in the market. The argument that training would be too late (Boswell 1973) ignores its investment nature. Without appropriate training the firm may survive, but its growth potential may be restricted. However, a number of problems regarding training have been highlighted:

(i) The lack of time available to the owner-manager for such training.
(ii) The quality of the training (Boswell 1973; Morris and Watkins 1982).
(iii) Which institutions should provide the training.

One source of training is professional advice, but there have been a number of criticisms about the quality of the infrastructure for the provision of advice to small businesses (Scase and Goffee 1980; Boswell 1973; Office of Fair Trading 1986; Bosworth and Wilson 1987). We note again that many of the subsidised advisory services, including local authorities, enterprise boards, the MSC, etc. have, historically at least, been aimed specifically at new firms rather than existing companies. Studies of government-funded centres for management training indicate a generally positive view about the assistance received (Howdle 1982), although there may be a need for a more extensive referral system and for a general extension of these services countrywide (Howdle 1982). It is argued that management training schemes still discriminate against women managers and that there are grounds for re-examining the conditions of entry onto agency courses (Watkins and Watkins 1986). Many studies argue that enterpreneurial training should be incorporated in the general education system (Scase and Goffee 1980; Haskins 1986), particularly in the case of groups such as engineers (Finniston 1980), who flow into management later during their careers (Venning 1979). Other European countries, Germany in particular, are far more involved with entrepreneurial training than Britain (Haskins 1986).

NOTES

1. The information reported about the Emilia Romagna region was presented by Mark Lazerson, Visiting Lecturer in the Department of Law, Warwick University, during an Institute for Employment Research Staff Seminar on 'Determinants of small business expansion in Emilia Romagna: the role of labour relations and market forces', 10/12/86.
2. See note 1 above.

REFERENCES

Anderson, T. and Warkov, S. (1961) 'Organization size and functional complexity: a study of administration in hospitals', *American Sociological Review* 26: 23–8.

Bain, S.G. and Elias, P. (1985) 'Trade union membership in Great Britain: an individual-level analysis', *British Journal of Industrial Relations*, 71.

Blanchflower, D. (1983) 'Unions' relative wage effects: a cross section analysis using establishment data', Discussion Paper No 106, Department of Economics, London: Queen Mary College.

Blandy, R., Dawkins, P., Gannicott, K., Kain, P., Kasper, W., and Kriegler, R. (1985) *Structured Chaos: the Process of Productivity Advance*, Melbourne: Oxford UP.

Boswell, J. (1973) *The Rise and Decline of Small Firms*, London: George Allen & Unwin.

Bosworth, D.L. (1981) 'The demand for qualified scientists and engineers', *Applied Economics* 13: 411–29.

Bosworth, D.L. (1987) 'Barriers to growth in small businesses: the labour market', Discussion Paper No 37, Institute for Employment Research, Coventry: University of Warwick.

Bosworth, D.L. and Dawkins, P.J. (1983) 'Work organization as a response to the employment implications of technological change', in Bosworth, D.L. (ed.) *The Employment Consequences of Technological Change*, London: Macmillan.

Bosworth, D.L. and Ford, J. (1985) 'Income expectations and the decision to enter higher education', *Studies in Higher Education* 10 (1): 21–31.

Bosworth, D.L. and Wilson, R. (1987) *Infrastructure for Technological Change*, Research Report, Institute for Employment Research, Coventry: Warwick University.

Brooks, J. (1971) *Business Adventures*, London: Pelican.

Burch, P.H. (1972) *The Managerial Revolution Reassessed*, Massachusetts: Lexington Books.

Byrt, W.J. and Masters, P.R. (1974) *The Australian Manager*, Melbourne: Sun Books.

Chevalier, J.M. (1969) 'The problem of control in large American corporations', *Anti-Trust Bulletin* 14.

Clutterbuck, D. and Devine, M. (1985) 'Why start-ups start', *Management Today*, July–Dec.

Clutterbuck, D. and Devine, M. (1985) 'The rise of the entrepreneuse', *Management Today*, January: 63.

Cross, M. (1983) 'The United Kingdom', in Storey, D.J. (ed.), *The Small Firm: an International Survey*, London: Croom Helm.

Cyert, R. and March, J. (1963) *A Behavioural Theory of the Firm*, New Jersey: Prentice Hall.

Dooley, P.C. (1969) 'The interlocking directorate', *American Economic Review* 59.

Eaton, J. (1985) 'Co-operative and new technology', *Industrial Relations Journal* 16 (4): 47.

Emery, F.E. and Phillips, C.R. (1976) *Living at Work*, Canberra: AGPS.

England, G.W. (1975) *The Manager and His Values: an International Perspective*, Massachusetts: Cambridge UP.

Finniston, Sir M. (1980) *Engineering our Future*, Cmnd 7794, London: HMSO.

Fleming, M.C. (1970) 'Inter-firm differences in productivity and their relation to occupational structure and size of firm', *Manchester School*, Sept.: 223–45.

Ford, G.W. (1983) 'Cultural differences in skill formation and the establishment of an Australian human resource office', *Manpower Planning and Industrial Development in Uncertain Times*, Sydney: ANZAAS.

Gibb, A. (1982) 'Small firms policy in Baden-Württemberg: some UK implications', in D. Watkins, J. Stanworth, and A. Westrip (eds) *Stimulating Small Firms*, Aldershot: Gower.

Gibb, A. (1982) 'The small-business institute programme in the USA and its relevance to the UK', in T. Webb, T. Quince, and D. Watkins (eds) *Small Business Research*, Aldershot: Gower.

Gill, J. (1985) *Factors Affecting the Survival and Growth of the Smaller Company*, Aldershot: Gower.

Hackman and Oldham (1980) *Work Redesign*, Massachusetts: Addison-Wesley.

Haskins, G. (1986) 'Small-business management training in European business schools and management centres', in M. Scott, A. Gibb, J. Lewis, and T. Faulkner (eds) *Small Firms Growth and Development*, Aldershot: Gower.

Howdle, J. (1982) 'An evaluation of the small firms' counselling service in the south west region', in T. Webb, T. Quince, and D. Watkins (eds) *Small Business Research*, Aldershot: Gower.

Institute for Employment Research (1986) *Review of the Economy and Employment 2*, IER Coventry: University of Warwick.

Institute for Manpower Studies/Occupations Study Group (1986) *UK Occupation and Employment Trends to 1990*, in A. Rajan and R. Pearson (eds) London: Butterworth.

Johnson, P.S. and Apps, R. (1979) 'Inter-locking directorates among the UK's largest companies', *Anti-Trust Bulletin*, Summer.

Katz, D. and Kahn, R. (1966) *Social Science of Organization*, John Wiley: New York.

Kotz, D. (1979) 'The significance of bank control over large corporations', *Journal of Economic Issues* 13.

Koutsoyiannis, A. (1975) *Modern Microeconomics*, London: Macmillan.

Kriegler, R.J. (1980) *Working for the Company*, Melbourne: Oxford UP.

Lansbury, R.D. and Spillane, R. (1983) *Organizational Behaviour: the Australian Context*, Melbourne: Longman Cheshire.

Lewis, J., Stanworth, J., and Gibb, A. (1984) *Success and Failure in Small Businesses*, Aldershot: Gower.

'Management development in the 1980s' (1985) in *British Institute of Management Report* Sept., 85.

Marris, R. (1964) *The Economic Theory of Managerial Capitalism*, London: Macmillan.

35

Marx, K. (1969) 'Technology as the prime mover of industrialization and social change', in T. Burns (ed.) *Industrial Man*, Harmondsworth: Penguin. (Excerpts from: 'A letter to P.V. Annenkov', 1846; Preface to *A Contribution to the Critique of Political Economy*, 1857 and *Capital*, 1867).

Melman, S. (1951) 'The rise of administrative overhead in the manufacturing industries of the United States: 1899–1947', *Oxford Economic Papers* 3: 61–112.

Minford, P. (1983) *Unemployment: Causes and Cures*, London: Martin Robertson.

Morris, J. and Watkins, D. (1982) 'UK government support for entrepreneurship training and development', in T. Webb, T. Quince, and D. Watkins (eds) *Small Business Research*, Aldershot: Gower.

Nelson, R.R. (1981) 'Research on productivity growth and productivity differences: dead ends and new departures', *Journal of Economic Literature* 19 (3): 1029–64.

Nelson, R. and Winter, S. (1974) 'Neoclassical vs evolutionary theories of economic growth', *Economic Journal* 84: 886–905.

Nelson, R., Winter, S., and Schuette, H. (1974) 'Technical change in an evolutionary model', *Quarterly Journal of Economics* 90: 90–118.

Nyman, S. and Silberston, A. (1978) 'The ownership and control of industry', *Oxford Economic Papers* 30.

Office of Fair Trading (1986) *Review of Restrictions on the Patent Agents' Profession*, London: OFT.

Penrose, E. (1959) *The Theory of the Growth of the Firm*, London: Blackwell.

Peters, T.J. and Waterman, R.H. (1983) *In Search of Excellence: Lessons from America's Best-Run Companies*, New York: Warner Books.

Pondy, L.R. (1969) 'Effects of size, complexity and ownership on administrative intensity', *Administrative Science Quarterly* 14 (1): 47–61.

Pym, D.L. (1971) 'Social change and the business firm', in D. Mills (ed.) *Australian Management and Society*, Melbourne: Penguin.

Radice, H.K. (1971) 'Control type, profitability and growth in large firms: an empirical study', *Economic Journal* 81.

Rainnie, A. and Scott, M. (1986) 'Industrial relations in the small firm', in J. Carran, J. Stanworth, and D. Watkins (eds) *The Survival of the Small Firm*, Aldershot: Gower.

Richie, J. (1986) 'Predictable casualties: the sacrificial role of the older small firm', in J. Stanworth and J. Curran (eds) *Management Motivation in the Small Business*, Aldershot: Gower.

Ritchie, J., Eversley, J., and Gibb, A. (1982) 'Aspirations and motivations of would-be entrepreneurs', in T. Webb, T. Quince, and D. Watkins (eds) *Small Business Research*, Aldershot: Gower.

Sargent, V. (1982) 'Large firm assistance to small firms', in J. Watkins, J. Stanworth, and A. Westrip (eds) *Stimulating Small Firms*, Aldershot: Gower.

Sawyer, M.C. (1981) *The Economics of Industries and Firms*, London: Croom Helm.

Scase, R. and Goffee, R. (1980) *The Real World of the Small Business Owner*, London: Croom Helm.

Stanworth, J. and Curran, J. (1986) 'Growth and the small firm', in Curran, J., Stanworth, J., and Watkins, D. (eds) *The Survival of the Small Firm*, vol. 2, Aldershot: Gower.

Stanworth, P. and Giddens, A. (1975) 'The modern corporate economy: interlocking directorships in Britain, 1956–70', *Sociological Review* 23.

Steer, P. and Cable, J. (1977) 'International organization and profit: an empirical analysis of large UK companies', Discussion Paper 77–47, Berlin: International Institute of Management.

Stewart, M. (1983) 'Relative earnings and individual union membership in the UK', *Economica* 50: 111–25.

Storey, D.J. (1982) *Entrepreneurship and the New Firm*, London: Croom Helm.

Storey, D.J. (1985) 'The problems facing new firms', *Journal of Management Studies*, May: 122–3.

Swords-Isherwood, N. (1980) 'British management compared', in K. Pavitt (ed.) *Technical Innovation and British Economic Performance*, London: Macmillan.

Thompson, J.D. (1967) *Organizations in Action*, New York: McGraw-Hill.

Toner, B. (1985) 'The unionization and productivity debate: an employee opinion survey in Ireland', *British Journal of Industrial Relations*, July.

Veblen, T. (1906) *The Theory of Business Enterprise*, Scribner.

Venning, M. (1979) *The Manager in Engineering*, Research Report No 7 Watford: Engineering Industry Training Board.

Watkins, D. and Watkins, J. (1986) 'The female entrepreneur in Britain: some results of a pilot study with special emphasis on educational needs', in M. Scott, A. Gibb, J. Lewis, and T. Faulkner (eds) *Small Firms Growth and Development*, Aldershot: Gower.

Westrip, A. (1986) 'Small firms policy: the case of employment legislation', in J. Curran, J. Stanworth, and D. Watkins (eds) *The Survival of the Small Firm*, Aldershot: Gower.

Wildsmith, J.R. (1973) *Managerial Theories of the Firm*, London: Martin Robertson.

Williamson, O.E. (1964) *The Economics of Discretionary Behaviour: Managerial Objectives in a Theory of the Firm*, New Jersey: Prentice Hall.

Williamson, O.E. (1967a) *The Economics of Discretionary Behaviour*, Chicago: Markham.

Williamson, O.E. (1967b) 'Hierarchical control and optimal firm size', *Journal of Political Economy* 75.

Williamson, O.E. and Bhargava, N. (1972) 'Assessing and classifying the internal structure and control apparatus of the modern corporation', in K. Cowling (ed.) *Market Structure and Corporate Behaviour*, London: Gray-Mills.

Wilson, P. (1982) 'Local authority assistance to small firms', in D. Watkins, J. Stanworth, and A. Westrip (eds) *Stimulating Small Firms*, Aldershot: Gower.

Wilson, R. (1984) 'The return on entering business professions', *The Business Economist*, Winter: 30–41.

Wilson, R. and Bosworth, D.L. (1986) *New Forms and Areas of Employment Growth*, Draft Final Report of the UK Study, Study No 85397 by the Institute for Employment Research for the European Commission: Brussels.

Woodward, J. (1966) *Industrial Organization Theory and Practice*, Oxford University Press: London.

ACKNOWLEDGEMENTS

We would like to thank Helen Rainbird for comments on an earlier draft of this chapter. The opinions expressed and the remaining errors are, however, the sole responsibility of the authors.

3

Lack of Finance as a Constraint on the Expansion of Innovatory Small Firms

Graham Hall

INTRODUCTION

The brief for our original report to ACARD was specifically to examine the state of knowledge on the extent to which lack of finance acts as a constraint on the expansion of innovatory small firms, but it has not been possible to focus it so precisely. The relationship of finance to innovation would appear to have been largely ignored in the literature. Matters are made worse by the common practice of writing as if the problems facing firms at birth can be regarded as synonymous with those of established small firms attempting to survive or with small firms intending to expand. Though the last is clearly the most pertinent to the purposes of this chapter, it has not always been possible to make even the elementary distinction between the problems of starting, surviving, and expanding.

It has been assumed that the primary interest of ACARD is in the extent to which small innovatory firms suffer disadvantages, compared to large firms, in their relationship to the capital market, and not in the far broader question of how far British industry is provided with adequate funds for investment. The evidence (Bain 1983; Prouse 1986) would appear to suggest that the rate of return earned in the non-oil sector has been, since 1973, below the real cost of capital, but a discussion of the reasons for this would need to include such diverse factors as the sociological reasons for different rates of saving between countries, the investment strategies of companies, and the macro-economic need for high interest rates.

The notion that the small-firm sector suffers from disadvantages in its relationship with the capital market has been popular for at least fifty years and was discussed by the Macmillan (1931), Radcliffe (1959), Bolton (1971), and Wilson (1979) Committees. These, and other writers, have all mentioned a 'gap' in the provision of finance to small firms but what precisely is meant by this often varies between authors and even between different parts of the same publication.

Various versions of what this gap might refer to would be:

(i) A difficulty in raising small amounts of capital, usually equity. The Macmillan Committee fixed on £200,000 as being the threshold figure in 1931.

(ii) Whilst there may not be a blanket minimum amount, below which it is difficult to raise, some viable small firms may unjustifiably suffer prejudice from the capital market. This prejudice may stem, for instance, from poor credit assessment procedures.

(iii) There may not be any difficulty facing small firms in raising money but they may be unfairly penalized, compared to large firms, in the interest they must pay, or security they must provide.

(iv) Small firms may suffer in their dealings with the capital market but this may be justifiable when seen from the perspective of the market. There would seem little doubt that small firms suffer a high casualty rate. Ganguly (1983) found that only 43 per cent of the businesses registered for VAT in 1973 survived the next ten years and it is not unreasonable to assume that the great majority of these businesses must have been small. Not surprisingly, the probability of its failure is inversely related to the size of a company (Hall and Stark 1986). Large firms are also able to bulk buy finance. The disadvantages, moreover, suffered by small firms may be in their financial management skills, rather than in inefficiencies on the part of the capital market.

(v) A gap may arise from the narrowness of the objectives of the capital market, particularly as regards the generation of employment. Jobs may be provided by small firms in spite of, or perhaps because of, low financial returns.

It is the intention of this chapter to review the state of our knowledge of the extent of these gaps. The format of the remainder of this chapter will be:

(i) The problems that are indigenous to small firms in their attempts to raise finance.

(ii) The adequacy of self-generated finance or that raised from friends or relatives.

(iii) The adequacy of the provision of finance to potentially expanding small firms from conventional clearing banks.

(iv) Finance from venture capitalists.

(v) Finance from other companies.

(vi) Finance from development agencies.

(vii) The results of various government schemes, in particular the Small Business Loan and Business Expansion Schemes.

(viii) The working of the Unlisted Securities Market.

(ix) The results of studies which have focused on the adequacy of finance for firms which are small but technologically orientated.

(x) A summary.

PROBLEMS INDIGENOUS TO SMALL FIRMS

Binks (1979) made two assertions as to the problems which are endemic to small firms:

(i) Increases in demand for their products occur in discrete steps of considerable size relative to turnover. Hence, turnover increases in sudden jumps rather than as a continuous process.

(ii) Increases in the supply of a firm's product often require outlays which are large in relation to its capital base.

Binks does not provide any evidence in support of these assertions, but as he was a researcher for the Wilson Committee, his impressions must be afforded some credibility. The second of the assertions would certainly appear plausible, merely being a re-affirmation of the lumpiness of many items of physical, or even human, capital. The validity of the first assertion, however, must surely depend upon the nature of the market in which the firms operate. If demand is diffused amongst a large number of customers its growth is likely to be more gradual than if demand is concentrated, though the increasing concentration amonst retailers will, admittedly, have a distorting effect on the demand experienced by producers.

The report by Robson Rhodes on companies applying for finance under the Small Business Loan Guarantee Scheme covered firms that were supposed to be marginal but its report makes

41

clear that applicants did not necessarily meet this criterion. Its assessment of the financial skills displayed by applicants is likely, therefore, to have more general applicability. The comments are damning. Unambiguously applicants possessed, on the whole, little or no idea of financial planning or control. This has been confirmed in discussions between the author of this chapter and a number of experts on small-business training. Such inefficiency must hamstring small firms in their negotiations with the capital market, not to mention increasing their likelihood of suffering failure.

FINANCE RAISED FROM PERSONAL RESOURCES AND FROM FRIENDS AND RELATIVES

The Wilson Committee, when examining the accounts of three hundred incorporated small firms, found 65 per cent of cash raised was internally generated. This, it argued, was an underestimate of the actual contribution made by owners as it ignored their injections of capital through loans and purchase of equity. The committee thought a more accurate estimate to be in the region of 75 per cent.

Binks and Vale (1984), in carrying out a survey of new small firms in the Nottingham area (differing, therefore, from the Wilson Study in geographical catchment area, age, and probably, size), found that of the forty three respondents who relied on single sources of finance, thirty raised the money from their own resources. Of the other fifty-seven respondents who had multiple sources, forty six had injected their own capital.

Though Binks and Vale's estimates were not weighted by value they would appear to confirm those of Wilson, i.e. internally generated capital is the most important source of capital for small firms, as indeed, it would be for large. We do not have similar statistics on small firms that have enjoyed expansion. In itself a bias towards internally generated capital does not serve as a commentary on the adequacy of alternative sources of finance. This would be reflected by the extent to which owners were required to make what might be considered unreasonably high personal contributions, either by way of security or from lack of alternatives. The former reason will be discussed further on page 44 but there is little evidence of the extent to which entrepreneurs are forced to rely on their own resources.

The Wilson Committee, and indeed Wilson himself in speeches made after the publication of its report, argued that a worrying decline had occurred in the amount of capital available from 'Aunt Agathas', i.e. private investors who knew personally the person they backed. One reason given for this alleged decline was the high rates of personal taxation and, to some extent, as a result of Wilson's recommendations, the Business Start-Up Scheme was initiated, which in 1983, was enlarged to form the Business Expansion Scheme. Ironically, parents, children and spouses of the owners of a business, any of whom might have been categorized as Aunt Agathas, were disqualified from providing investments under the scheme. Its effectiveness will be discussed on page 51.

Though it would seem plausible that the importance of Aunt Agatha, in real terms, or relative to other sources of capital, has declined, whether this is of the scale implied by Wilson is an open question. Binks and Vale (op. cit.) offered some support to Wilson in that eight of the hundred companies in their sample had been given or lent money by friends and relations.

FINANCE FROM CLEARING BANKS

According to the Wilson Committee, in 1975, bank overdrafts represented 12 per cent of the total liabilities of small companies, against 10 per cent of those of large companies. The clearing banks are the principal vehicle by which entrepreneurs can compensate for the shortfall in their ability to generate internally all the capital they might require. Banks have been criticized for:

(i) Charging small firms too much.
(ii) The level of security required.
(iii) Being conservative in their attitude as to the purposes for which they will make loans.
(iv) Being inefficient in their procedures of credit assessment.

The Wilson Committee claimed that small firms were charged a 2 per cent higher rate than that paid by large firms. There would seem little doubt that this premium persists but might be defended as reflecting:

(i) The greater probability of failure within the small-firm sector.

(ii) The fixed-cost element in assessing an application for a loan.

(iii) The buyer-power exerted by large customers.

These arguments are a little undermined by the results of a study by Churchill and Lewis (1985) of the costs and revenues of the various activities of an American bank. Though its loans in total to small businesses were costlier and riskier than those to large, they produced more deposits and were overall more profitable.

The Wilson Committee not only criticized banks for the rate of interest they charged but for the level of security they demanded. It claimed that, whilst a 1:1 gearing ratio was fairly common in Britain, European banks were often prepared to accept 2:1 or even 3:1. Similarly the security ratios required, that of net assets to borrowing, were in the 2:1 to 4:1 range. Of the twenty-five firms on which Binks and Vale were able to be very precise, fifteen had to meet ratios of over 2:1. Moreover, almost two-thirds of their sample had to provide, as security, their house, a personal guarantee, or their insurance policy.

Banks do not publish data on the segmentation of their market as regards the breakdown by size of their customers or the length of the period for which their loans are made, but discussions between the author and managers from the national offices of the major clearing banks would suggest that *ceteris paribus* the younger and smaller the company the less willing would be a bank to enter into a long-term commitment and the more anxious to limit its activities to the financing of working capital. This impression is confirmed by the tone, and by specific comments, of the reports by Robson Rhodes (1983a, 1983b, and 1984). It would seem that the conservatism of local bank managers – matters may possibly be different at regional offices – leads them to prefer short, arm's-length relationships, monitored through bank statements, in which the minimum amount of money is involved. The last point is particularly important as entrepreneurs are, of necessity, natural optimists in their expectations as to how little capital they might need. The result, Robson Rhodes (1984, p. 83) argued, was that, 'many of the businesses we have studied have been under-financed. The under-financing of a new business starts it as a cripple'.

Within clearing banks, senior branch bank managers often have the authority to make fairly large loans, say up to £500,000, without the need to refer their decision to their regional office. Though there does not appear to be a great deal of evidence on how bank managers or, even less, their colleagues in regional or central offices carry out their appraisals, what little there is would appear to be very damning. The Robson Rhodes report (1984), in particular, is scathing in its criticisms of branch managers. A large proportion of the applicants under the Small Business Loan Guarantee Scheme were not required to supply even the most fundamental information. Bank managers were 'either not skilled in appraising business propositions . . . or continue to rely on the traditional standards of character and capital: the man as distinct from the business' (p. 77). It was not that managers were less careful, because the government was prepared to underwrite 80 per cent of the loan, but rather (p. 81) Robson Rhodes found, 'limited technical expertise amongst branch managers in analysing business propositions'.

The review of the literature on appraisal methods published by the NEDC (1986a) is not overtly so critical but, in reporting the suggestions for improvements appearing within the literature, serves only to highlight the current inadequacies of the appraisal process. What is largely neglected is a strategic analysis of the position of an applicant firm in relation to market conditions and competitor behaviour. This case should not be overstated, however. Centres of training of senior management in British banks, most notably Manchester Business School, do attempt to broaden the perspectives of their students, but in the face of conservatism.

THE VENTURE CAPITAL MARKET

The venture capital market represents an important source of externally generated equity for small firms seeking to expand. This section will:

(i) Define the market
(ii) Describe its activities
(iii) Assess its adequacy
(iv) Suggest areas for further research

Venture capitalists are characterized by a willingness to:

45

(i) Provide long-term investments in equity-finance, though loans may also be included in the package.

(ii) Take their gains in terms of the changing value of their capital, rather than in dividend or interest repayments.

(iii) Take risks, though this certainly does not imply that security is not required for loans, or that preference shares will not be included in the equity package.

(iv) Take a long-term interest in the company. This can take the form of an involvement in the business, and implies an absence of the hands-off relationship normally characteristic of the quoted sector.

(v) Make investments in the small to medium-sized, almost certainly unquoted, corporate sector.

There are currently over a hundred UK venture capitalists. According to Lorenz (1985) ten years ago there were only twelve, and thirty years ago, two. Hardly surprisingly, whilst writers disagree quite markedly as to the actual figures, there can be no doubt that there has been a dramatic increase in the volume and value of investments made by venture capitalists. A NEDO report (1986) estimated that in 1982 venture capitalists made 321 UK investments with a total value of £110 million and in 1984, 569 investments valued at £228 million.

There is again quite marked divergence of opinion as to the precise breakdown but, for the sake of consistency, if nothing else, it is perhaps appropriate to quote the NEDO estimates that in 1984, 43 per cent of investors were 'captive', i.e. part of a larger organization, whilst about 25 per cent were private independent funds. A fifth were Business Expansion Scheme funds, which will be discussed below, and the balance consisted of a few publicly listed funds and government- or local-authority-backed investors (also discussed below).

Government initiatives such as the BES, and the provision in the 1981 Companies Act to allow companies to buy back their shares, a recommendation made by the Wilson Committee facilitating easier exit by investors, undoubtedly played a part in stimulating the venture capital industry, but it would seem likely that a more important reason lay in the belief, particularly within the major financial institutions, that the small-firm sector represented a previously missed opportunity for speculative gains, and that the future, especially in certain high-technology areas, lies with this sector.

In spite of the growing importance of venture capitalism it would appear to contain a number of serious weaknesses:

(i) In spite of their claim to serve the small-firm sector, venture capitalists are very unwilling to invest at below £100,000 and usually the threshold is £250,000. Whether these amounts are consistent with those required for expansion by innovatory small firms is an open question.

(ii) Though venture capitalists are quick to claim their willingness to take risks, they are far from undemanding in their criteria for making investments. The NEDO report cited rates of 2 per cent or 3 per cent successful applications as being typical.

(iii) Though venture capitalists would seem, *prima facie*, the appropriate source of finance for innovatory firms, there is some evidence that they are shifting the balance of their portfolios towards the possibly safer service sector. In 1983, the computer-related sector comprised 27 per cent of the total amount by value invested, and other electronics businesses a further 24 per cent; a year later the amounts were 17 per cent and 13 per cent respectively.

(iv) There would appear to be a strong bias from venture capitalists in favour of London and the South East (*UK Venture Capital Journal* 1986). Over 60 per cent of venture capital companies are based in London and between them they accounted for more than 75 per cent of the total amount invested in 1985. Though they appear more willing than their regional counterparts to invest throughout the country, nevertheless 60 per cent of the companies they financed were located in their area.

(v) A survey of venture capitalists in the Manchester area, made as part of a cost-benefit study of Greater Manchester Economic Development Corporation (Berry, Hall, and Lewis 1986) does not suggest the venture capital market to be particularly open. Business appraisal executives usually appear familiar with the investments being considered by their competitors and have expressed reservations about investing in companies already turned down by one of them.

If we know a little about the appraisal techniques of the clearing banks, we know nothing about those of venture capitalists. They claim a high level of expertise but whether this is true must remain, until research is undertaken, a matter of conjecture. Given the importance of this sector in providing the finance necessary for the expansion of innovatory small firms, such research would appear to be recommended.

COLLABORATION WITH SMALL FIRMS

Sometimes called corporate venturing, collaborative relationships between large and small firms represent, in the United States, an important source of venture capital. Hickman *et al.* (1985) estimate it at approximately 20 per cent of such capital. In the UK, however, they have identified seven companies that are engaged in corporate venturing and a further three that have done so in the past. Given that this figure is so surprisingly low, a question mark must hang over whether this represents an accurate estimate of the total UK population of firms that are, or have been, involved in this activity. In our examination of corporate venturing we will:

(i) Discuss the forms that corporate venturing can take.
(ii) Describe the corporate venturing activities within the UK.
(iii) Draw some lessons for the success of this activity from the US experience.

The source throughout is Hickman *et al.*, op. cit., who wrote their report for NEDO as part of their MBS MBA programme.
The forms that corporate venturing can take in the United States are:

(i) *External venture fund:* the corporation invests in a professionally managed fund. This represents a low risk but provides few spin-offs from the innovative skills of the investees.
(ii) *Internal venture fund:* the corporation establishes its own fund as an autonomous unit to provide a window on new technology.
(iii) *Direct investment 'hands off':* the corporation makes a direct investment in an entrepreneurial company and, at least initially, allows it a free-hand.
(iv) *Direct investment 'hands-on':* here the corporation provides some degree of managerial assistance as well as finance.
(v) *Spin-offs:* as a by-product of its R&D efforts, a corporation may develop an idea on technology that does not fit its mainstream interest but which nevertheless would seem worth

developing. It may, therefore, opt to exploit its idea through a separate company.

(vi) *Joint ventures:* this represents a simple pooling of resources and is most common where large firms assist in the international marketing of the innovations of the smaller partner.

(vii) *Internal venturing:* this arises where an individual or group within a corporation is provided with total responsibility for a product and is allowed to run its division in isolation from the rest of the corporation.

Apart from a firm which wished to remain anonymous, Hickman *et al.* listed British Steel, British Petroleum, Ferranti, ICI, Pilkingtons, and Thorn EMI as undertaking corporate venturing, usually through an internal venture fund.

The average size of the venture fund of the five companies that were prepared to provide details was £3.5 million. Not including those by British Steel, Hickman *et al.* estimated thirty ventures are currently being undertaken, with quite marked variations in the proportions of equity stake. Since 1981, British Steel has made well over nine hundred investments, apparently mainly through unsecured loans.

Hickman *et al.* visited several companies in the US involved in some way in corporate venturing and drew a number of lessons for companies considering following the same route and for a government anxious to assist them. Amongst these were:

(i) The best results from internally managed funds or divisions will probably be achieved with the minimum of interference from the rest of the company.

(ii) Corporate venturing can provide valuable information on potential areas of high growth.

(iii) It would appear that British law is less favourable than American to the incorporation of venture funds.

FINANCE FROM DEVELOPMENT AGENCIES

The Wilson Committee recommended that an English Development Agency be established, with similar powers to its Scottish and Welsh counterparts. Whilst this was not adopted, several local authorities set up regional agencies, usually called enterprise boards. We will look at these agencies' development banking activities and assess their effectiveness.

This section is based on Hall and Lewis (1987). In 1987 the nine agencies Hall and Lewis considered had total investment funds of just over £200 million and had invested a little over half of this in approximately 4,000 businesses.

The agencies claim to attempt to plug two important gaps in the capital market since:

(i) They are usually prepared to provide packages of equity and loans to small companies, including start-ups.

(ii) They usually adopt a wider perspective than the purely financial in their evaluation process, most notably the number of jobs that will be directly or indirectly generated.

Hall and Lewis have two major criticisms of the performance of agencies:

(i) They have not grasped the nettle that non-financial criteria in decision-making imply lower financial returns. Hence agencies are attempting to be all things to all men.

(ii) Plugging a gap in the market implies avoiding areas of overlap. Agencies rarely adopt the principle of additionality, making investments in companies that would otherwise not be favourably received by the commercial capital market and only maintaining, in their portfolio, sufficient high-return companies to ensure overall viability.

THE EFFECTS OF GOVERNMENT SCHEMES

Companies may receive financial assistance from central or local government under a variety of schemes which are not specifically connected with their size or degree of innovation but which, none the less, would enable them to expand. It would be quite beyond the scope of this discussion to review all such schemes, details of some of which are provided in a report published by the Bank of England and City Communications Centre (1985). This section will focus on:

(i) The British Technology Group, the work of which would appear pertinent to small innovatory firms.

(ii) The working of the Business Expansion Scheme.

(iii) The working of the Small Business Loan Guarantee Scheme.

The British Technology Group, comprising the National Research Development Corporation and the National Enterprise Board, has, as its objective, the promotion of the development of new technology into commercial products. It can provide finance to companies that want to develop their products and processes based on new technology. BTG can provide up to 50 per cent of the funds required for a project, and will expect to recover its investment by means of a levy on sales. The group can also provide equity to launch a new science-based company.

The author has found no assessment of the work of BTG, and indeed, very little knowledge by experts in this area, even of its existence.

The Business Expansion Scheme (Knowlman 1985) was established to encourage equity investment in small, high-risk companies. Amounts of £500 to £40,000 can be invested annually by individuals in companies undertaking various, specified activities, but money cannot be withdrawn for a minimum of five years. In return for this, tax relief is offered at the highest rate. BES capital can be raised through the twenty-six managed funds (1983/4) or directly from investors. It would appear about an equal amount of money was raised from both sources but that the average direct investment was smaller than those made through the managed funds. Within a year of being introduced in 1983 approximately four hundred companies had benefited from BES investments, about 28 per cent of which were in consumer-related activities, 11 per cent in industrial and the balance in electronics.

A number of criticisms may be levied at its operation so far:

(i) The average size of the amounts received from funds was £160,000, and 90 per cent were above £100,000. Only direct investments, constrained by the provisions of the scheme, were made in amounts of £40,000 or less.

(ii) There would appear to be a distinct regional bias in the working of the scheme, with 42 per cent of its funds being channelled into the South East.

(iii) High-technology firms may be constrained from exploiting the scheme because it specifically forbids investees from operating subsidiaries in the United States.

(iv) The mechanics of the scheme do not appear to be running very smoothly, with delays of up to two years for tax rebates.

51

The Small Business Loan Guarantee Scheme was introduced in 1981, as a result of a recommendation of the Wilson Committee, to compensate for the bias, justified or otherwise, displayed by the capital market towards small firms. Under the scheme the government underwrote 80 per cent of a loan made by a bank. The intention was that the loan would not have been made in the absence of this guarantee. By 1984, 13,000 loans had been approved under the scheme.

Robson Rhodes, in its reports on the scheme (op. cit.), was not very flattering about the appraisal process applied by banks but was far more circumspect about whether the scheme was in general worthwhile, and more particularly, whether the principle of 'additionality' had been observed. The tone of its reports was that banks had often misused the scheme to underwrite the loans that they would have provided anyway, and to remedy this Robson Rhodes suggested the guarantee be reduced to 70 per cent. This suggestion was adopted.

In attempting to provide evidence on the extent of additionality they estimated that 47 per cent of finance could have been secured in the absence of the scheme if respondents had been prepared to look hard for an investor, whilst in 34 per cent of cases this would, in fact, have occurred. They might equally have cited the failure rate amongst beneficiaries under the scheme. As this was no worse than amongst small firms in total, either the firms were not marginal or the credit assessment, normally applied by banks, is clearly not very reliable at filtering out potential failures.

THE UNLISTED SECURITIES MARKET

The USM represents the mechanism by which the more successful small firms can achieve a significant injection of external equity through flotation, though larger firms may prefer the USM to the Stock Exchange on which they would be required to offer at least 25 per cent of shares for sale.

Between 1980 and 1984, 329 companies joined the USM, of which 41 subsequently joined the Stock Exchange. Based on Hansrod (1985) our description of the companies which opted for listing on the USM is as follows:

(i) Of the 269 companies still on the USM at the end of 1984, 57 were in the electricals industry, 55 in miscellaneous manufacturing, 22 in leisure, 20 in gas and oil, and 19 in drapery and stores.

(ii) Of the 71 in electricals that had actually joined the USM (gross of failure or movement to the Stock Exchange) 45 were suppliers or distributors of computer accessories, hardware, software or computer service-orientated activities.

If the 6 electronic security system companies are added, high-technology firms represented 72 per cent of the electricals. Companies from electricals equalled 27 per cent of those graduating to a full listing on the Stock Exchange and most of these were in computer-related activities.

(iii) In 1984, the average turnover of USM listed companies = $12 million (48 per cent < £5 million), with:

average capital employed = £6 million (50 per cent < £3 million);

average return on capital employed = 20 per cent

average liquidity ratio $\dfrac{\text{liquid assets}}{\text{liquid liabilities}} = 1.78$

compared to 1.05 for Stock Exchange listed companies

(iv) A cash-flow analysis would suggest a major reason for seeking a listing was to sustain a capital investment programme, rather than to satisfy the need for short-term liquidity.

Hall and Hutchinson are currently in the process of analysing the results of an econometric study on the factors associated with small firms achieving a listing on the USM during the 1980s and those that were floated on the Stock Exchange during the 1970s.

Their conclusions are tentative and provisional but would suggest that whilst relative growth rates remained the most important discriminator between firms that did, and did not, achieve a listing, a surprising shift has occurred over time in the relationship of profitability and of directors' own income/sales to the probability of achieving a listing.

Hutchinson and Ray (1983) have considered various aspects of small firms that were floated on the Stock Exchange during the period up to 1973. They found no evidence to suggest that such firms or a control group of non-floated companies, had previously suffered particularly badly at the hands of the capital market. Rather they shifted the emphasis to the need for small firms to implement appropriate control systems to monitor performance.

In January 1987 the Stock Exchange introduced the Third Market, intended to attract investors who had shown interest in the small speculative companies traded on the USM and the unofficial over-the-counter market. Three months later it was not showing the amount of activity that was originally hoped (*Financial Times*, 27.4.87) with an average of £2.18 million worth of business being carried out on average each week. Clearly, it is too early to draw any conclusions about its usefulness.

FINANCE AND INNOVATION

As so little has been written specifically about the extent to which the growth of innovative small firms is inhibited by its relationship to the capital market, it is perhaps worthwhile to pay a little attention to the results of two recent projects which have focused on this topic.

Oakey (1984) reported the results of a survey of owners of small companies, located in the south east of England or in Scotland, who were producing scientific instruments or electronic components. These were:

(i) High-technology firms were more likely than low-technology firms to fund their investments externally.

(ii) Innovative firms were more likely to have been refused a bank loan. Oakey concludes from this that bank managers are not competent to value the output of R&D.

(iii) A third of firms which raised their capital principally from external sources had previously been refused a bank loan; in other words in spite of, rather than because of, the banks' attitudes they eventually succeeded in raising the necessary capital. This reflects the general tone of the article.

(iv) There would appear to be a superior take-up of government technology-related schemes in Scotland than in the South East.

NEDC (1986b) conducted a postal survey of small to medium-sized firms in the electronics sector and, through consultants, interviewed a sample located in the South East, from those who had responded to the initial survey. Assuming no bias from ignoring non-respondents, it would appear that:

(i) Firms in their early development stage generally prefer to raise external capital in the form of debt rather than equity. This the NEDC ascribed partly to companies' ignorance about the role of equity, and partly to the difficulties of raising equity in amounts below £100,000.

(ii) Only just over half of the companies that raised their external finance through equity were impressed by the institutions' understanding of their business, but NEDC thought the blame lay with companies' ignorance about the extent that some institutions had specialized in electronics, as much as with some institutions' lack of understanding of the problems of the sector.

(iii) Companies relying on loans often found banks to be excessively conservative in their attitudes to risk, frequently requiring personal guarantees as security.

(iv) In so far as any clear message is evident from the report, it is that the capital market does not fully understand the problems endemic to firms that are innovative, but that these firms cannot entirely escape blame in their understanding of the needs of financial institutions.

SUMMARY

There is little doubt that, compared to large firms, small firms are usually required to pay a higher rate of interest and offer a higher level of security. This reflects, partly, the greater risk inherent in the small-firm sector and, partly, the endemic conservatism of bank managers. The latter, furthermore, are inefficient at undertaking financial appraisals.

(i) There is a definite equity-gap, certainly in terms of the amounts that can be readily raised from external sources and, possibly, in terms of the assessment procedures that are applied by venture capitalists.

(ii) There are currently only a handful of British companies undertaking corporate venturing.

(iii) Local development agencies, on a very modest scale, would appear to be entering a gap within the services provided by venture capitalism.

(iv) The Business Expansion Scheme is clearly of benefit but a question mark hangs over its total effectiveness.

(v) A significant number of investments, made under the Small Business Loan Guarantee Scheme, would probably have occurred in its absence.

(vi) The USM represents a useful mechanism for injecting equity finance into companies that are fast-growing, often technology-based and medium-sized.

Some weak evidence suggests that the capital market is an inhibiting force on the growth of innovative firms but not necessarily cripplingly so.

Areas that should be the subject of further research are:

(i) The extent that potentially viable firms are denied the finance necessary to grow. In spite of all the material cited, we have no idea of the number of companies affected by inefficiencies in the capital market.

(ii) The assessment procedures employed by venture capitalists.

(iii) The effects of differences between the provisions offered by the capital markets within Britain's competitors on the ability of their innovative small firms to reach their full potential.

REFERENCES

Bain, A.D. (1983) 'The Wilson Report: three years on', *Three Banks Review* 138.
Bank of England and City Communications Centre (1985) *Money for Business*, London: Bank of England.
Berry, A.T., Hall, G.C., and Lewis, P. (1986) *A Cost Benefit Study of GMEDC*, Report to the Ten North West Districts.
Binks, M. (1979) 'Finance for expansion in the small firm', *Lloyds Bank Review*, October.
Binks, M. and Vale, P. (1984) 'Finance for the new firm', *NUSFU Paper 2*, University of Nottingham.
Bolton, J.E. (1971) *Small Firms: Report of the Commission of Inquiry on Small Firms*, Cmnd 4811, London: HMSO.
Burns, P. and Dewhurst, J. (eds) (1986) *Small Business in Europe*, London: Macmillan.
Churchill, N.C. and Lewis, V.L. (1985) 'The profitability of small business lending', *Journal of Bank Research*, Summer.
Dewhurst, J. and Burns, P. (1983) *Small Business: Finance and Control*, London: Macmillan.
Fletcher, S.J., Kirby, M.E., and Morley, N.J. (1985) 'The UK venture capital market', *MBA Marketing Project MBS*.
Ganguly, P. (1983) 'Lifespan analysis of business in the UK, 1973–82', *British Business*, 12 August 1983.
Hall, G. and Lewis, P. (1987) 'The need for, and effectiveness of,

development banking by regional development agencies', *MBS Working Paper 147*.

Hall, G. and Stark, A. (1986) 'The effects of the Conservative Government as reflected in the changing characteristics of bankrupt firms', *International Journal of Industrial Organisation*.

Hansrod, A. (1985) 'The cost and financial performance of new issues on the unlisted securities market', MBSc dissertation, MBS.

Hickman, M., Lynch, J., Pervez, A., Stonier, J., and Street, P. (1985) 'A study of corporate venturing in the UK', *A Government Business Relations Project Report*, MBS.

Hutchinson, P.J. and Ray, G.H. (1983) *Financing and Financial Control of Small Enterprise Development*, Aldershot: Gower.

Knowlman, N. (1985) 'Business expansion scheme', MBS MBA dissertation.

Lorenz, T. (1985) *Venture Capital Today*, New Hampshire: Woodhead-Faulkner.

Macmillan Committee (1931) *Report of the Committee on Finance and Industry*, Cmnd 3897, London: HMSO.

NEDC (1986a) *Lending to Small Firms*, A report prepared by Doran, A. and Hoyle, M. of the Economists Advisory Group.

NEDC (1986b) *Finance for Growth*.

NEDO (1986) *Venture Capital in the UK and its Impact on the Small Business Sector*, paper prepared for NEDO by John Chapman.

Oakey, R.P. (1984) 'Finance and innovation in British small independent firms', *OMEGA* 12: 2.

Prouse, M. (1986) 'The key to competitiveness', *Financial Times* 28 October.

Radcliffe Committee (1959) *Report of the Committee on the Working of the Monetary System*, Cmnd 827, London: HMSO.

Robson Rhodes (1984) *A Study of Business Financed Under the Small Business Loan Guarantee Scheme*, London: DTI.

Robson Rhodes (1983a) *An Analysis of Some Early Claims Under the Small Business Loan Guarantee Scheme*, London: DTI.

Robson Rhodes (1983b) *Small Business Loan Guarantee Scheme – Commentary on a Telephone Survey of Borrowers*, London: DTI.

UK Venture Capital Journal (1986) 'Special report: regional venture capital', September.

Wilson Committee (1979) *The Financing of Small Firms: Interim Report of the Committee to Review the Functioning of the Financial Institutions*, Cmnd 7503, London: HMSO.

4

Barriers to Growth:
The Labour Market

Derek Bosworth

SUMMARY

While technological change implies the need for subsequent changes in the education and skill structure of the firm, changes of this type are also a prerequisite for innovation and growth.

Labour costs per employee increase with firm size. Several reasons have been offered for this, including the non-pecuniary benefits of working in small firms. However, the primary explanations are probably the higher utilization of labour (i.e. hours of work and shiftworking) and the greater quality of labour in large firms. While it cannot be conclusively proven from the labour cost data alone, there may be some size below which the costs of growth outweigh the benefits (i.e. a size at which some discrete switch to a more advanced technology becomes possible). What is clear, however, is that, other things being equal, the higher costs per employee will act as a disincentive to growth.

Part of the rise in the labour cost per employee can be traced to differences in the mix of manual to non-manual workers in firms of different sizes. However, both categories of worker exhibit increasing costs per employee (even though the non-manual curve is 'flatter'). Thus, there are changes in the extent of utilization and the quality of the workforce, even holding the manual/non-manual mix constant.

Both wage and non-wage labour costs per employee increase with firm size. A number of non-wage costs can be viewed as a tax on the firm, bringing no direct benefits, and acting as a barrier to growth. In so far as these non-wage costs include quasi-fixed labour costs, they alter the firm's choice between persons and hours, reducing the size of employment (and raising the utilization of labour). Both arguments are consistent with the growing view that unemployment can be reduced by lowering employer NICs.

There are direct links between the capital intensity, level of technology and skill structure of the firm. In order to develop and grow, smaller firms face the problems of raising the quality and level of expertise of their workforce. Failure to do so leaves the firm vulnerable in the face of changing market conditions and further technological advances amongst larger competitors.

In recent years, increasing emphasis has been placed on the role of education and training in growth. While most of this debate has been at a more aggregate level, there are important analogies between the under-achieving nations and small firms.

The ability to adopt, adapt, and assimilate technical and organizational innovations depends on the quality of both the entrepreneur and the workforce. The crucial role of investments in labour force competence are now beginning to become clear from the empirical literature. However, small firms are least able/least willing to attract high-quality personnel, although there is a tendency for the small-business owner-manager to under-estimate the quality of his existing workforce.

Such problems might manifest themselves in terms of shortages of vital skills. However, these appear to be more apparent in larger and technologically more dynamic concerns. The explanation appears to be two-fold. First, inadequacies may not be registered in so far as they can be traced primarily to the small-firm owner-manager him/herself. Second, shortages are ephemeral: actual shortages become latent, assimilated by the lowering of aspirations and targets.

Small firms not only begin from a lower-quality base, but they are also disadvantaged in their ability to carry out training programmes. They undertake less training per employee and it seems likely that, pound for pound, the training is less productive than in larger firms. The small firm is also forced to make more use of informal rather than formal training. Where formal training is undertaken, they are forced to make more use of external sources which seem likely to have a lower 'firm-specific' content. The net result is that the training does not 'lock' the employee within the small firm, and this lowers the return to training. These problems are compounded by the lower returns to training investments funded by individual workers, accentuating the overall under-investment in training activity in small firms.

Small firms have less well-developed internal labour markets (partly as a result of their lower training). Their greater need for flexibility means that they are more often forced into the external labour market. One response has been the adoption of a core-periphery workforce, where adjustment takes place primarily through the peripheral workforce. Peripheral workers blur the distinction between internal and external adjustment, reducing adjustment costs. They also enable the small firm to maintain a higher quality of workforce than would otherwise be the case. On the other hand, the higher ratio of periphery to core reduces the average quality of the workforce below that of larger firms. The questions of how peripheral workers can be trained and how the training can be funded appear likely to become increasingly important issues as this component of the labour force continues to grow.

Small firms are less unionized than their larger counterparts. While unions are unlikely to resist growth *per se*, nevertheless, they are afraid of both the labour-saving nature of the technological change that is the vehicle for growth and the loss of control over the work that the new technologies often imply. Little evidence of resistance can be found either in the national union pronouncements on technological change or in the survey results of the barriers to innovation. On the other hand, there are a number of specific examples of resistance in particular firms and industries. However, a number of such examples appear linked to the 'adversarial' approach adopted in announcing or introducing the new technology.

A number of items of labour market legislation have affected the small-firms' choice between workers and hours, as well as their preferred method of adjustment. The existence of a size limit up to which firms are exempt from certain legislation produces a threshold, which may restrict firms' growth.

TECHNOLOGY, HUMAN CAPITAL, AND GROWTH

A central premise here is that, in general, a more rapid diffusion of new technology within any given organization will produce faster growth (Nelson and Winter 1978; Pavitt and Soete 1980; Barras and Swann 1983; Stoneman 1984; Wilson 1984; Whitley and Wilson 1986), a view embodied in the 'success breeds success' hypothesis (Nelson and Winter 1978, p. 541). For the innovating organization, the substitution of capital for labour will to some degree, perhaps wholly, be offset by the expansionary effects of the growth in demand for the firm's output (Stoneman 1984). These arguments are consistent with the empirical tests based on Verdoorn's Law (Kaldor 1966; Wabe 1974; Smith *et al.* 1982, pp. 52–5; Kaspura and Ho-Trieu 1980; Metcalf and Hall 1983). A major theme of this chapter is that the success of technological and organizational innovations depends crucially on the human capital of the firm. While it is widely recognized that innovation implies the need for subsequent changes in education and skills, this paper emphasizes that such changes may be a prerequisite for innovation and growth. The sort of firm we have in mind would typically have less than 50 employees and is currently in operation (i.e. as opposed to a new start-up). While the firms in question might be either higher- or lower-technology, it is assumed that neither type is achieving the rapid growth that might be hoped for.

ABSOLUTE LABOUR COSTS

The fact that wages and salaries per employee per hour increase with plant and firm size is well documented: for example, size is an important explanatory variable in earnings functions (Bosworth and Wilson 1987a), although it may be a proxy for other influences related to size, such as overtime and shiftwork (Wabe and Leech 1978, p. 305; Bosworth and Wilson 1987b and 1987c). Data from UK labour cost surveys[1] show the extent of such differences. The data from this source are reported by size of establishment (rather than by size of firm), although, in the main, small establishments are also small firms. For example, taking the ratio of each size category to the results for the 10–49 group, in 1984 labour costs per employee were 11.1 per cent higher in the 50–99 category, 12.2 per cent higher in the 100–199 category, 18.5 per cent higher in the 200–499 size range, 32.4 per cent higher in the 500–999 category, and 42.8 per cent higher in the greater than 1,000 size. The main features of the labour cost/size relationship are illustrated by the upper line in Figure 4.1. This type of relationship can be found across almost all industries for which the data are published. This is illustrated in Figure 4.2 using information from the chemicals and textiles industries.

In general, there are good reasons for the increases in labour cost per employee that take place, otherwise, other things being

61

Figure 4.1: Labour cost by establishment size

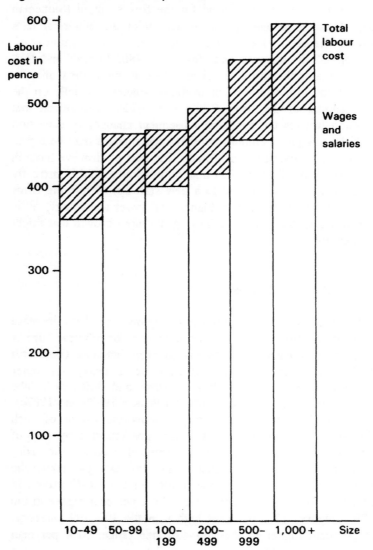

equal, all firms would remain small. In other words, larger firms reap the rewards of higher labour productivity, which offset the costs of the higher labour cost per hour. However, for this to take place, small and larger firms must be qualitatively different. The point that we would make is that it is possible for small firms to survive in a low-technology, low-wage (often lower-profit)

Figure 4.2: Labour cost of manual workers by establishment size in chemical and textiles industries

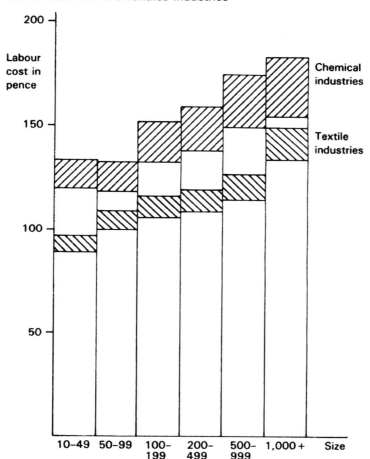

environment, alongside larger firms in a high-technology, high-wage (often higher-profit) environment. A necessary stimulus for growth in the small-firm sector is that profits are higher in the high-technology and higher-wage situation. If we assume that this is the case, then the essential question concerns the problems posed by the transition from small to large. In principle, by examining whether there is any particular establishment size at which labour costs per employee suddenly exhibit a discrete 'jump', it is possible to explore if there is some obvious size barrier at which this qualitative change takes place (and, therefore, growth may be inhibited). In practice, for a variety of reasons which we will touch on, the isolation of transitional barriers of this type may be problematic, although a more sophisticated empirical treatment could be revealing.

The cost data for 1984 suggest a marked shift in per unit labour costs at the smallest size level (although we would not want to make too much of this result, for reasons outlined below). The movement from a mid-range size of 30 to 75 (somewhat greater than doubling of size) produces an 11 per cent increase in per unit labour costs. The doubling of mid-point size from 75 to 150 produces only a 1 per cent increase. On the other hand, the movement from 150 to 350 (slightly more than doubling) produces a 5.6 per cent increase, and the subsequent moves from 350 to 750 and from 750 to over 1,000 produce 11.8 and 7.8 per cent increases. However, while per unit labour costs rise with establishment size, the relationship appears quite complicated. First, the function is not always monotonic and has changed over time (as the labour market, taxes and subsidies, etc., have altered). Second, from an analytical perspective, the relationship poses a number of currently unanswered questions, for example: why do individuals supply themselves to smaller firms when they pay less and, conversely, why are larger firms willing to pay more?

We leave the first of these questions to future research; however, it is perhaps worth exploring the second of these in somewhat more detail. One argument is that non-pecuniary factors make smaller firms more attractive, thereby increasing supply and lowering the wage. On balance, however, it appears unlikely that this could cause such a major differential: a study of male shop-workers found lower fringe benefits, little support for the old theory that relationships are closer and warmer, and higher labour turnover in small firms (Curran and Stanworth 1981). The lower wage may also be the result of a lower average age of workers in smaller enterprises (Curran and Stanworth 1981). However, the principal factor is almost certainly the lower quality of the workers hired, which is linked to the different organizational and technological strategies of smaller firms (discussed in detail below and in Bosworth and Jacobs 1987).

COSTS AND THE MANUAL/NON-MANUAL WORKFORCE

Differences in cost partly reflect the changing mix of manual and non-manual workers in firms of different sizes (Bosworth and

Wilson 1987a and 1987b). The labour cost survey indicates that non-manual wage and salary costs per person per hour were 34.5 per cent higher than for manual workers. 'On costs' are also higher, and non-manual labour costs per person per hour were 39.1 per cent higher than for manual workers. However, the explanation cannot be wholly attributed to a change in the manual/non-manual ratio, as per unit labour costs increase with firm size for both categories of workers. In 1975, for example, labour costs per manual employee for each successive size establishment compared with the 10–49 category were: 3.2 per cent higher in the 50–99 category; 9.5 per cent higher in the 100–199 category; 15.6 per cent higher in the 200–499 category; 23.7 per cent higher in the 500–999 category; and 42.9 per cent higher in the greater than 1,000 category. The analogous comparisons for non-manual workers were as follows: 5.8 per cent (50–99); 7.0 per cent (100–199); 7.5 per cent (200–499); 14.3 per cent (500–999); and 28.9 per cent (greater than 1,000). Despite the 'flatter' curve, labour cost per non-manual employee is still significantly higher in larger than smaller establishments. Thus, the higher labour costs amongst both categories of employees, coupled with the need to increase the proportion of non-manual workers, may act as a barrier to growth amongst cost-conscious employers. The fact that both labour cost curves increase with size indicates that other influences are at work, including changes in other dimensions of the quality of the workforce.

STRUCTURE OF LABOUR COSTS

Data from the labour cost survey indicates the changing structure of labour costs over time. The proportion of wages and salaries in the total shrank from 91.8 per cent in 1964 to 87.5 per cent in 1975 and then to 82.3 per cent in 1983. Within this total, the proportions attributable to statutory national insurance and voluntary social welfare contributions approximately doubled between 1964 and 1983 (from 3.6 to 7.5 and 3.1 to 6.1 per cent respectively). The other costs category showed an even larger increase, from 1.5 to 4.1 per cent. Thus, increases in real wages have been augmented by the growth in non-wage labour costs. 'On costs' have formed the subject of considerable debate in Australia, where their growth threatened the prevailing prices and incomes policy, the so-called 'Accord' (Dawkins and Blandy 1985). Research suggests that the growth in quasi-fixed labour costs (one element of 'on costs') has caused substitution of hours for employees (Ehrenberg 1972; Hart and Sharot 1978) and reduced employment. Parallel work suggests that lower unemployment could be achieved by reducing employer NICs.

Data from the labour cost survey indicate that non-wage labour costs form a smaller proportion of total labour costs in smaller firms, even though wages and salaries per employee are lower in smaller firms than in larger firms. The relationship for all manufacturing is illustrated in Figure 4.1 and for chemicals and textiles in Figure 4.2. In manufacturing firms in 1984, wages and salaries formed 86.4 per cent of total labour costs of all employees in the 10–49 category, compared with 82.7 in the greater than 1,000 category. The detailed breakdown of the non-wage element of labour costs for all manufacturing in 1980 is illustrated in Figure 4.3. Only two categories of labour costs other than wages and salaries decrease in relative importance with establishment size: liability insurance and employers' statutory national insurance contributions. The former is relatively small (0.5 per cent of per unit labour costs in the 10–49 category and 0.2 per cent in the greater than 1,000), while the latter is more important (8.4 per cent in the smallest category and 7.1 per cent in the largest). Redundancy provision (0.3 to 2.0 per cent), voluntary social welfare payments (3.2 to 5.9), benefits in kind (0.1 to 0.2), subsidized services (1.1 to 1.6), and training (0.1 to 0.4) all increase.

The fact that larger establishments tend to have higher per unit 'on costs' may form a barrier to growth, particularly where these costs do not yield direct benefits to the firm in question. There are important differences in the structure of UK labour costs and those of European competitors (SOEC 1981a, 1981b): for example, in the percentages going to both employers' statutory social security contributions and other labour costs (e.g. training). Expenditure by UK firms on training is known to be low and this influence on our ability to compete has come under increasing scrutiny in recent years (see pp. 77–9).

Figure 4.3: Structure of non-wage labour costs

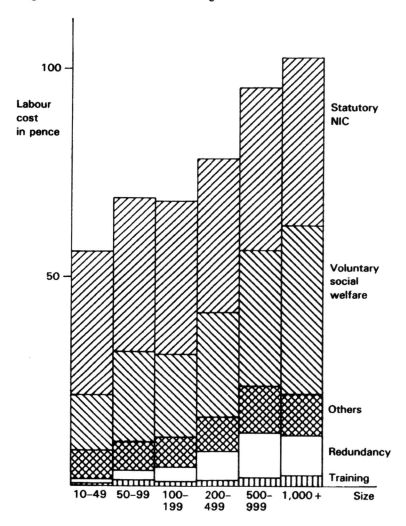

TECHNOLOGY, SKILL STRUCTURE, INNOVATION, AND GROWTH

Growth by means of increasing the number of workers without any other changes within the company (i.e. in the capital stock) is likely to be extremely limited. Traditional economic theory of the returns to one factor suggests that productivity increases as the fixed stock of capital is used more efficiently, but then declines and even becomes negative if employment is expanded too far (Tangri 1966). The principle that workers in larger firms can become more specialized and, thereby, through the process of learning by doing (more and longer), become more productive has been recognized since Adam Smith, and manifests itself in Taylorism. Specialization requires a demarcation between jobs and this, in turn, involves the firm in job redesign, co-ordinating the actions of man and machine, and influences the organizational structure within which the worker operates. Specialization creates problems for smaller firms, resulting in the need to subcontract specialized work where the capacity of a person embodying a particular skill cannot be fully utilized. Such services are not always appropriate to the small firm and can prove costly, as in the case of specialist patenting skills (Bosworth and Wilson 1987a). Barriers of this type can be removed by: internal growth; provision of 'shared facilities'; a shift away from Taylorism (discussed at length in Bosworth and Jacobs 1987).

In the UK, smaller firms are generally less capital-intensive and less technologically advanced (i.e. machines, robots, etc., tend to be concentrated in larger establishments – Bosworth *et al.* 1988), although, in other economies (such as the Emilia Romagna region of Italy), many small firms are as close to the technology frontier as their larger counterparts.[2] Relatedly, larger UK firms are also more skill-intensive and their labour productivity is significantly higher (Melman 1956; Fleming 1970). There is a direct relationship between firm size and the density of highly qualified technological manpower involved with the dynamic performance of the firm. In 1965, for example, professional engineers and technologists formed 0.4 per cent of employees in manufacturing establishments with 11–49 employees compared with 1.2 per cent in those with more than 500. Similar differences existed for professional scientists (0.2 to 0.6) and technicians (3.2 to 6.3) (Committee on Manpower Resources for Science and Technology 1966). Larger firms also allocate a significantly larger proportion of HQTM to R&D. The relationship between firm size and R&D is well documented (Freeman 1982, pp. 199–206).

Imitation of a recently introduced technology might necessitate further advances before adoption can take place (Griliches 1960a and 1960b). The organization's ability to introduce new products or processes will depend crucially on the ability of its workforce, including its management, to suggest and to assimilate these changes. Project SAPPHO, for example, highlighted the key role of entrepreneurship, strong enough to effectively co-ordinate R&D, production, and marketing (Freeman 1982). The SEFIS study of CNC innovation in small companies highlighted the role played by directors, often with an engineering background, who carried out the programming and, later, trained someone from the shop floor to do this work (Research Associates 1984, p. 19). Case-study evidence of three companies in the food industry showed that the management's attitudes towards training and, thereby, the extent and nature of the training determined the success of the introduction of new technology (Cross and Mitchell 1986). A lack of spare managerial capacity or ability can prove an important barrier to growth in small firms. For further discussion of the role of management see Bosworth and Jacobs (1987).

While management plays a crucial role, the overall quality of the workforce is also important to the 'capacity to adapt itself to the requisites of advanced technology and to adapt the advanced technology to its own circumstances and objectives' (Solo 1966). The crucial role of labour in the process is only now beginning to be captured in empirical work: for example, Johansson and Karlsson (1985) conclude that, 'adoption of new technologies is strongly influenced by labour force competence and network properties of individual establishments' and, thereby, 'in investments in labour force competence'. While earlier work has often stressed the role of highly qualified labour in the dynamic process (Bosworth and Wilson 1978; Finniston 1980; Bosworth 1981a and 1981b), more recent work in a number of countries has also focused on the role of intermediate skills (Prais 1981; Prais and Wagner 1983; Daly *et al.* 1985; Lawrence 1984; EITB 1972, 1975; TSA undated; EITB/MSC 1986).

The results outlined above are consistent with the rate of return to education and the economics of production and growth literatures, which highlight the important contribution of the quality of the workforce. The economics of education literature is based on the premise that, with positive rates of return, more training will lead to higher productivity and output (Blaug 1968, 1969, 1972). The literature on education, production and growth includes studies of the residual factor (Schmookler 1952; Kendrick 1961; Solow 1957) and the contribution of education to growth (Schultz 1960, 1961, 1963; Griliches 1970; Denison 1962, 1964, 1967; Kendrick and Grossman 1980; Finniston 1980). More recent evidence, often at the plant level, highlights the importance of training in the comparative growth performance of, for example, the UK and German economies (Prais 1981; Prais and Wagner 1983; Daly *et al.* 1985; Lawrence 1984). Again, there are analogies here with the comparative performance of firms. Training is clearly a means of avoiding actual and latent skill shortages (or reducing skill surpluses). It is a means of improving the human capital of the workforce that allows the optimal utilization of existing productive capacity, and the introduction of new products and processes (Food and Drink Industry EDC 1983; Rainbird and Grant 1985, pp. 12–13). However, the two dimensions of growth and quality of the work-force are likely to be interrelated and jointly determined (Nelson 1981, p. 1055; Blandy *et al.* 1985, pp. 40–1).

In principle, when a firm is first established, it can recruit the most able people (i.e. those with the most appropriate intellect, skills, experience, education). The evidence of the labour cost data is that small firms are least able (or perhaps least willing) to attract such people. Certainly, they seem likely to face higher recruitment costs in the external labour market, at least for the more formal methods of recruitment. Even if they were able to attract these people in the first place, the subsequent growth of the firm is likely to depend crucially on the development of its human capital. The SEFIS I study found most owners 'amazed at the ability of the men on the shopfloor, especially the younger men, to adapt and learn new methods. There was occasionally scepticism among the older men, but most were willing to learn, albeit at a slower pace' (Research Associates 1984, p. 19). Managers of small firms may underestimate the fund of ability that they have within the firm. Certainly, the CNC technology appeared to be introduced quickly and with few hitches by the SEFIS I adopters, although the self-selection for the scheme and the high level of supplier and government support may have conspired to produce a favourable outcome.

The results presented in this section are largely consistent with the evidence on labour costs (see pp. 61–7). In essence, most small firms opt for a low-technology route, in terms of both their capital and labour. While they also experience lower productivity, they also experience lower per unit capital and labour costs, which allow them to compete with the larger, higher-technology firms. On the other hand, it also leaves them vulnerable to varia-tions in product prices and to further technological advances in the high-technology sectors, because they are ill-equipped to improve their technology and may be forced to look for still lower-quality and lower-priced labour. It seems likely that the small firm is a microcosm of the British economy: to grow it must move from lower to higher levels of technology, productivity and value added (Bosworth *et al.* 1988). Not least of the barriers is for the firm to accept that growth will involve employing higher-quality inputs (both capital and labour) and incurring higher per unit factor costs.

SHORTAGES OF QUALIFIED MANPOWER

Studies focusing on factors retarding the introduction of new technology have found a significant role for labour shortages, for example, 'shortages of skilled manpower to implement and maintain the equipment' (Wilson 1984, p. 40). A study of the factors slowing the introduction of microelectronics in the UK manufacturing sector pointed to the 'lack of people with microelectronics expertise' as the predominant hindrance in both product and process applications (Northcott and Rogers 1982). A survey undertaken in 1983, in conjunction with similar organizations in Germany and France, confirmed the importance of lack of expertise in the UK (Northcott *et al.* 1985). The authors note that:

> The sort of person most crucially in short supply seems to be a professional engineer with training and expertise in microelectronics hardware and enough knowledge also of software and of the other kinds of engineering needed for the product to be able to lead a design team to develop a new product or introduce a new production process.

In a study of the diffusion of microelectronics in south-east England, Bourner *et al.* (1983, p. 106) also emphasize the importance of having the appropriate skills available within the firm. There were few differences between large and small firms, although, if anything, a greater proportion of larger firms suggested problems associated with lack of available skills. The principal reason appears to be that, 'the shortage of people with relevant expertise is felt most, not in the more backward establishments . . . but in the larger ones, in the more technologically advanced and complex applications' (Northcott *et al.* 1985, p. 35). The results indicate that there are two distinct types of shortage: actual shortages, where the firm is experiencing some problem because of their current or planned activities; latent shortage where, because firms are reconciled to lower-level technology and slow growth, they effectively avoid such shortages by default. This concept of latent shortages underpins the Finniston (1980) thesis of a shortage of engineers, when all current indicators showed no signs of significant excess demand (Bosworth 1981a; Bosworth and Wilson 1980). The argument is also to some extent consistent with the finding that firms in Germany and France both rated skill shortages a more important factor than in the UK, even though Germany, for example, 'appears to have the highest rate of applications of the three, and . . . a strong tradition of technical training in industry' (Northcott *et al.* 1985, p. 35).

TRAINING AND SIZE

Anecdotal evidence of a lack of training in small firms that hinders growth is now more fully supported by empirical results (Curran and Stanworth 1981). This is not immediately apparent when firm size is measured in terms of turnover and when the commitment to training is measured as expenditure on training as a proportion of turnover (Industrial Society 1985, p. 3): 85 per cent of companies with turnovers of £51–100 m spend less than 0.5 per cent of their turnover on training, compared with 82 per cent of firms with turnover in the £101–500 m range. On the other hand, a larger proportion of some of the smaller companies spent *more* than 0.5 per cent of their turnover on training: 67 per cent with a turnover of less than £5 m, 43 per cent of those with a turnover of £6–25 m and 52 per cent of those in the £26–50 m category. This result may be somewhat misleading, however, as larger establishments tend to have a higher capital/lower labour intensity. Thus, the same source indicates that the percentage of turnover allocated to training increases with firm size, when firm size is measured in terms of numbers of employees (Industrial Society 1985). Amongst the respondents, none of the 6 firms with less than 100 employees spent more than 0.5 per cent of their turnover in this way, while 42 per cent of firms with more than 10,000 employees spent more than 0.5 per cent of turnover. The changes in the proportion of turnover devoted to training did not increase wholly monotonically with employment size, but this would seem to be a result of the relatively small sample size of this survey.

Bearing in mind, therefore, that training expenditure per employee is perhaps a better measure of the intensity of training activity, there is considerable evidence that larger firms undertake more intensive training. The labour cost survey data show that expenditure per employee was higher for larger establishments than for smaller (Department of Employment *Gazette*, November 1977, Tables 10 and 11, see pp. 61–4 above). In 1975, for example, the expenditure per manual worker formed 0.1 per cent of average hourly labour costs in the 10–49 size category, 0.3 per cent in the four size categories up to 1,000 employees and 0.4 per cent above 1,000 employees. A similar pattern of training expenditure emerged in the case of non-manual workers, except that the percentage rose more steeply from 0.1 per cent of labour costs amongst the smallest size category to 0.4 per cent in the categories that fell in the 200–999 range, while the largest establishments, with over 1,000 employees, spent a slightly lower proportion of labour costs, at 0.3 per cent. This result is again supported by EITB data on the costs of training technicians and technician engineers (EITB 1975, p. 13). In this instance, average gross training costs per technician were lower in the 100–199 than the 250–499 group in every year of training. The costs net of productive work tended to accentuate this result even further, particularly in the earlier years of the programme of training.

As might be expected, most of the firms undertaking training employed both internal and external training, although external was used more widely than internal (Industrial Society 1985, p. 5). The ratio of internal to external increases with firm size: while only 44 per cent of firms with a turnover of less than £5 m employed internal training, 97 per cent of those with £101–500 m turnover and 91 per cent of those with £501 m turnover or more did so. While there is no direct evidence from the survey, it might be hypothesized that internal training contains a higher 'specific' and lower 'general' training component (Becker 1964). The sample size also restricts the amount of information published on which types of employees receive the training, and there is no firm size detail for this. However, it is interesting to note that management training was cited by most firms (96.7 per cent), with technical and professional and secretarial and clerical equal second (quoted 89.3 per cent of firms (Industrial Society 1985, pp. 6–8). Manual workers and apprentice training were quoted significantly less. The percentage of training budget allocated to each of these occupational categories tended to reinforce this finding, with management receiving the highest and manual workers the lowest percentages amongst those companies undertaking training for these groups of workers.

The discussion indicates a number of key reasons why small firms undertake less training per employee than larger firms. First, they are more labour-intensive, so a given training budget (even fixed as a percentage of turnover) is spread more thinly per employee. Second, the returns to training, and the willingness of firms and individuals to fund it, are affected by the lower level of specialization of employees in smaller firms and by the associated lack of development of an internal labour market. Third, the balance of 'specific' to 'general' training is likely to be related to the ratio of internal to external training, and thereby to firm size. The more general nature of the training in small firms, therefore, fails to help to lock employees into the firm, and this reduces the rate of return to this type of investment. Fourth, labour turnover is anyway likely to be higher in smaller firms (Curran and Stanworth 1981), not only because of poorer training, but also because of lower pay and other conditions of work, and this reduces the willingness of small companies to train. Fifth, small companies are relatively high-risk employers with higher insecurity of employment, and this reduces the willingness of individuals to fund their own training, accentuating the results based on firm expenditure data. Finally, in so far as training is characterized by increasing returns to scale, the positive differential in training received by individuals in larger firms may be augmented by its higher productivity (as in the case of activities such as R&D: Fisher and Temin 1973).

Small firms seem less able or willing to attract higher-quality employees, in part because of the low level of training on offer, coupled with the relatively low level of technology. However, even if small firms set off from a fairly high-quality base, their lower level of training places them at an increasing disadvantage over time. Current trends in self-employment and the casualization of the workforce (Atkinson 1984, 1985; Wilson and Bosworth 1986), particularly amongst the smaller firms, suggest new difficulties in maintaining and increasing the skill level of the workforce. To some extent the experience of the construction industry, with an important small and medium-sized firm sector and relatively mobile, although often skilled, labour force, could be used to gain insights (Rainbird and Grant 1985, pp. 65–85). The implication of this, therefore, is that if small firms want to instigate a virtuous circle of higher-technology products and processes, coupled with higher-quality labour, and thereby grow, they will have to find some new mechanisms for improving the extent and quality of the training on offer.

INTERNAL AND EXTERNAL LABOUR MARKETS

All firms need to adjust their levels of labour services in response to changes in market conditions. Size for size, the extent of the adjustment in small firms is likely to be larger in so far as they face greater product market movements, more competitive situations and higher labour turnover at any given point in the cycle. The small firm therefore has a need for greater flexibility in both the internal (ILM) and external (ELM) labour markets. In essence, ELMs focus on the firm's search for labour outside of its own organization; ILMs are concerned with the movement of labour *within* the organization. ELMs and ILMs emerge at the 'port of entry', generally at the bottom of some promotional ladder; above this point they diverge because the ILM is an administrative unit isolated from external market forces (i.e., the pricing and allocation of labour services are governed by a set of administrative rules and procedures, and different wage and employment outcomes emerge) (Dunlop 1966).

Internal adjustment can take place through changes in hours of work and worker effort. The extent of adjustment in both of these is bound by the physical limits on their supply from the existing workforce, as well as by the disproportionate increases in their cost at the margin both above and below 'normal' utilization levels. The former is associated with high overtime and PBR premia, and the latter by guaranteed pay, and more general wage-efficiency considerations are relevant to both directions of adjustment. The greater variability of demand suggests that, other things being equal, the small firm will be forced out into the external labour market more frequently than the large firm (we return to this below). It also suggests that there is an incentive for the small firm to take evasive action, to lower the internal costs of adjustment within the firm. One method is to remain small enough to avoid both formalizing the pay structure and trade union involvement.

A second and related method is to adopt a 'core-periphery' approach, where adjustment tends to take place through part-time, casual and home workers (Hakim 1985; Blanchflower and Corry 1985), where premia rates and guaranteed pay are not applicable. Given the links between such workers and the black economy (Wilson and Bosworth 1986), this strategy may reduce the apparent size of the firm. It also blurs the distinction between internal and external labour market adjustment, as such workers maintain their links with the firm even when they have no work. It is not clear that this 'casualization' lowers the quality of the workforce below what it might otherwise be, as the 'core-periphery' strategy maintains a body of expertise within the core that might otherwise be lost by other forms of adjustment. On the other hand, this strategy reduces the average quality of small vis-à-vis large firms, as the latter, on average, are likely to have a higher ratio of core to periphery.

ILMs are more relevant to large rather than small organizations (Whitehead and Baruch 1981, p. 90), as they are linked to product market power, skill specificity of the workforce (Becker 1964; Doeringer and Piore 1971), the extent of on-the-job training and the need for rules and procedures to overcome control loss (Williamson 1967). ILMs offer reduced turnover, lower hiring costs, known training to standards, greater worker learning and experience of both tasks and the firm organization, etc., which translate themselves into gains for the individual (i.e. 'career jobs' and steeper age-earnings profiles) and for the firm (i.e. higher productivity and product quality). Larger size may be a pre-requisite for the development of an ILM, on the other hand, particularly in so far as ILMs offer competitive advantages, their development may also be a prerequisite of growth. The growth of the small firm almost certainly implies a transition from the use of ELMs to ILMs. The development of an ILM requires the establishment or evolution of both formal and informal systems of management (see Bosworth and Jacobs 1987). In addition, the divorce from direct market forces may allow bureaucratic and uncompetitive practices to creep in, leading to inflexibility in responding to external pressures for change, particularly when formalized within trade union rules and contracts of employment. The bureaucratic nature of ILMs, based on rules and procedures, in part involving formal systems of management, may be very alien to the typical small-business owner-manager.

Other things being equal, the greater variability of product demand and the generally more precarious position of small firms implies that they will be driven into the ELM more frequently.

The employment function (Bosworth and Dawkins 1989, Chapter 9) and job search (Holt and David 1966; Phelps 1971; Diamond 1984) literatures suggest that hiring and firing are expensive activities, and adjustment takes time. The difference in frequency suggests that this activity will be qualitatively different amongst small firms. They appear more likely to use low-cost, informal methods of search. These cost considerations are probably reinforced by the owner-manager's preference for informal management (see Bosworth and Jacobs 1987). The low-cost option, however, is more appropriate to lower skill levels and is likely, other things being equal, to result in lower-quality workers. We noted earlier that peripheral workers help to blur the distinction between internal and external adjustment. In addition, while peripheral workers may have a relatively high turnover, they, nevertheless, fit quite well within this low-cost ELM option, unlike more highly experienced and qualified core workers. Clearly, until the firm can grow sufficiently in size to develop ILMs and bind its more experienced workers to it, the firm tends to be forced towards this relatively low-cost/low-quality option.

TRADE UNIONS, TECHNOLOGY, AND GROWTH

In the main, trade union representation is lowest in the smallest companies. The small-firm owner-manager might well be reluctant to grow to a size where unionization becomes an issue (see Bosworth and Jacobs 1987). Where unions already exist, it seems unlikely that they will directly resist growth, except in so far as it reduces union power. However, a prime mover of growth is technological change, and the unions might, in principle, resist labour-saving technological change.

At the national level, union views have tended to be pro-innovation. It has been argued, for example, that, 'resisting technological change . . . would be a recipe for general impoverishment, low growth and high unemployment. Improving the productive capacity of industry . . . should be a major priority for all trade unionists' (APEX 1979, p. 13). It has been pointed out that many trade unions actively encourage their members to ensure that their employers adopt new technologies in order to increase their firm's competitive position (James 1983, p. 175). What seems to be at issue is the control of the new technology (TGWU 1978, p. 3) and, the related question, of who benefits from it (James 1983, p. 175). The benefits may be in the form of better job security; higher pay; reductions in the working week, year and lifetime, etc. (although less so for those displaced) (TUC 1979).

Bamber (1986, pp. 3–9) stresses the difference between general, often national-level, union *policies*, which may reflect 'long-held ideological orientations', and union *responses* in the face of the introduction of new technology. Union responses may take a variety of forms, ranging from participative involvement (which is generally accepted as the most successful approach to innovation) through to complete resistance. The response depends on a variety of factors. First, there are a number of cultural and social factors, including the traditional adversarial posture amongst unions in English-speaking countries (Bamber and Lansbury 1984) and the tendency for UK employers to negotiate *ex post*. Second, on the nature of the innovation in terms of: the number of jobs affected; changes in the degree of skill required; changes in the types of skills required; how well the new technology is understood; etc. (Slichter *et al.* 1960; James 1983, p. 176). Other fears surround the way in which the new technologies might make jobs less amenable to worker control, for example, where a reduction in the range of tasks carried out makes the individual worker's performance easier to measure (APEX 1980, p. 32). Third, it depends on the state of the product market, with higher levels of competition and an expanding market to produce a greater willingness to accept the new technology (op. cit.). Fourth, it also seems certain to depend on the labour market environment, although the factors at play to some extent operate in opposite directions: union power tends to be increased during tight labour markets, but resistance is reduced when other jobs are relatively abundant (Hunter *et al.* 1970; Bamber 1986, p. 10). Finally, response will depend on the make-up, organization, structure, etc. of the trade union itself. A study of the transport industry suggested that the union was more likely to accept the change if: it had a broad membership base; was large in size; was politically secured with a stable leadership; was not involved in inter-union rivalry; there was a concentration of power within the union; it was faced by employer unity; its members were offered higher pay to match the higher post-innovation productivity (Levinson *et al.* 1971).

Questionnaire survey evidence of the importance of various hindrances to the adoption of new technologies tend to rate trade union opposition as relatively unimportant. A number of studies have indicated that, if anything, trade union attitudes towards the introduction of NC machines and microelectronics tend to be more favourable in the UK than in other countries, such as France and West Germany, although perhaps less so than in the USA (Nasbeth and Ray 1974, p. 56; Northcott *et al.* 1985, p. 72). This hypothesis about union attitudes is consistent with US evidence that labour productivity is higher in the unionized sectors (Brown and Medoff 1978; Freeman and Medoff 1979). The evidence collected about small firms participating in the SEFIS I scheme suggested that the CNC technology was 'welcomed' by the majority of workers, who generally recognized that the security of their jobs depended on their firm adopting the new technology before their rivals did so. Indeed, this seemed to be the primary benefit for the workforce, because, the report notes, 'In most cases the new CNC equipment was manned by skilled operators and treated as just another machine, with no special status or pay adjustment involved. Sometimes apprentices were used' (Research Associates 1984, p. 19). Whether this would be the case in other small companies or in larger, unionized concerns is subject to doubt: the report noted that, 'unions became evident in companies employing more than 100 and negotiation was often necessary to assuage fears of new machinery replacing jobs' (op. cit., p. 19). It is clear from other evidence that, at least in a number of UK industries (i.e., the steel, cotton-spinning, and printing industries), that trade unions may reduce the rate of introduction of new technology (Elbaum and Wilkinson 1979; Lazonick 1979).

GOVERNMENT EMPLOYMENT LEGISLATION

A number of pieces of government employment legislation may have affected the potential growth of companies, in part through their impact on labour costs. In particular, the Factories Acts, the Redundancy Payments Act (1965), the Sex Discrimination Act (1975), etc. all have their implications for costs of the firms that are subject to the legislation. Small firms have often been exempt from the legislation (i.e. firms with under five employees were exempt from the provisions of the Sex Discrimination Act, 1975). Thus, the limits of firm size for exemption may provide an upper limit to the size of the 'official' labour force of the firm. Further growth may take place through sub-contracting and the casualization of the workforce, rather than in-house. For example, the provisions of the Redundancy Payments Act (1965) were in some instances avoided by insuring that workers did not remain in 'official' employment for a sufficiently long period to qualify for severance pay (i.e. two years). The implications for the development of human capital essential to both the success and growth of the company and the life-cycle development of pay for the individual may be extremely important. The growth in youth training schemes of various kinds, including YTS, may have affected firm size in a number of ways. Not least of these is that YTS workers are generally not classed as employees of the firm (Dutton 1986).

NOTES

1. All data on this topic are taken from the 'Labour costs' surveys, in particular: 'Labour costs in GB, 1973', *Gazette*, September 1975, 873–85; 'Labour costs in GB, 1975: analyses for manual (operatives) and non-manual (administrative, technical, and clerical) workers', *Gazette*, November 1977, 1221–38; 'Labour costs in 1978', *Gazette*, January 1981, 12–21; 'Recent trends in labour costs', *Gazette*, October 1982, 447–9; 'Recent trends in labour costs, 1981 to 1984', *Gazette*, July 1985, 280–3; 'Labour costs in 1984', *Gazette*, June 1986, 212–18. All references are to the Department of Employment, HMSO: London.
2. Based on information presented by Mark Lazerson (Visiting Lecturer, Department of Law, University of Warwick) at an Institute for Employment Research Staff Seminar on 'Determinants of small business expansion in Emilia Romagna: the role of labour relations and market forces', 10/12/86.

REFERENCES

APEX (1979) *Office Technology: the Trade Union Response*, London: APEX.
APEX (1980) *Automation and the Office Worker*, London: APEX.
Atkinson, A.J. (1984) 'Emerging UK network patterns', in *Flexible Manning: the Way Ahead*, Sussex: Institute for Manpower Studies, Report No. 88.
Atkinson, A.J. (1985) 'The changing corporation', in Clutterbuck, D. (ed.), *New Patterns of Work*, Aldershot: Gower.
Bamber, G. (1986) 'Technological change and unions', paper presented to Group C: Skills, Labour Markets and Union Strategy, *Trade*

Unions, New Technology and Industrial Democracy Colloquium, 6–8 June, Coventry: University of Warwick.

Bamber, G. and Lansbury, R. (1984) 'Industrial relations and technological change: towards a comparative typology', paper presented to the *European Regional Congress*, October, Vienna: International Industrial Relations Association.

Barras, R. and Swann, J. (1983) 'Information technology and the service sector: quality of services and quality of jobs', in Marstrand, P. (ed.), *New Technology and the Future of Work and Skills*, London: Frances Pinter.

Becker, G.S. (1964) *Human Capital: A Theoretical and Empirical Analysis, with Special Reference to Education*, Princeton: Princeton University Press.

Blanchflower and Corry (1985) *Part-Time Employment in Great Britain: An Analysis using Establishment Data*, Report to the Department of Employment, Coventry: Institute for Employment Research, University of Warwick.

Blandy, R., Dawkins, P., Gannicott, K., Kain, P., Kasper, W., and Kreigler, R. (1985) *Structured Chaos: the Process of Productivity Advance*, Melbourne: Oxford University Press.

Blaug, M. (1968) *Economics of Education 1*, Harmondsworth: Penguin.

Blaug, M. (1969) *Economics of Education 2*, Harmondsworth: Penguin.

Blaug, M. (1972) *An Introduction to the Economics of Education*, Harmondsworth: Penguin.

Bosworth, D.L. (1981a) 'Technological manpower', in Lindley, R. (ed.), *Higher Education and the Labour Market*, Guildford: Society for Research into Higher Education.

Bosworth, D.L. (1981b) 'The demand for qualified scientists and engineers', *Applied Economics* 13: 411–29.

Bosworth, D.L. and Dawkins, P.J. (1983) 'Innovations in work organization as a response to the employment implications of technological change', in Bosworth, D.L. (ed.), *Employment Implications of Technological Change*, 208–23, London: Macmillan.

Bosworth, D.L. and Dawkins, P.J. (1989) *Labour Economics*, London: Longmans (forthcoming).

Bosworth, D.L., Dutton, P.A., and Green, A. (1988) *Review of the Engineering Industries*, Research Report, Coventry: Institute for Employment Research, University of Warwick (forthcoming).

Bosworth, D.L. and Jacobs, C. (1987) 'Barriers to growth in small businesses: management attitudes, behaviour, and abilities', Discussion Paper No. 36, Coventry: Institute for Employment Research, University of Warwick.

Bosworth, D.L. and Wilson, R.A. (1978) 'Some evidence on the productivity of qualified manpower in Britain: a note', *Bulletin of Economic Research* 30: 45–9.

Bosworth, D.L. and Wilson, R.A. (1980) 'The labour market for scientists and technologists', in Lindley, R. (ed.), *Economic Change and Employment Research Policy*, London: Macmillan.

Bosworth, D.L. and Wilson, R.A. (1987a) 'Shiftwork and developments in pay since 1973', in Gregory, M. (ed.), *Developments in Pay in the*

1970s, Oxford: Oxford University Press (forthcoming).

Bosworth, D.L. and Wilson, R.A. (1987b) 'Hours of work and developments in pay since 1973', in Gregory, M. (ed.), *Developments in Pay in the 1970s*, Oxford: Oxford University Press (forthcoming).

Bosworth, D.L. and Wilson, R.A. (1987c) *Infrastructure for Technological Change*, Research Report, Coventry: Institute for Employment Research, University of Warwick.

Bourner, T., Davies, H., Litner, V., Woods, A., and Woods, N. (1983) 'The diffusion of microelectronics in south-east England', in Bosworth, D.L. (ed.), *The Employment Consequences of Technological Change*, 97–109, London: Macmillan.

Brown, C. and Medoff, J. (1978) 'Trade unions in the production process', *Journal of Political Economy* 86(3): 355–78.

Committee on Manpower Resources for Science and Technology (1966) *Report on the 1965 Triennial Manpower Survey of Engineers, Technologists, Scientists and Technical Supporting Staff*, Cmnd 3101, London: HMSO.

Cross, M. and Mitchell, P. (1986) 'Packaging efficiency – the training contribution', discussion paper, London: Technical Change Centre.

Curran, J. and Stanworth, J. (1981) 'The social dynamics of the small manufacturing enterprise', *Journal of Management Studies*, 18(2): 141–58.

Daly, A., Hitchens, D.M.W.N., and Wagner, K. (1985) 'Productivity, machinery, and skills in a sample of British and German manufacturing plants', *National Institute Economic Review*, February 1985, 48–61.

Dawkins, P.J. and Blandy, R. (1985) 'Labour costs and the future of the Accord', *Australian Economic Review* 11.

Denison, E.F. (1962) 'The sources of growth in the United States and the alternatives before us', Supplementary Paper No. 13, New York: Committee for Economic Development.

Denison, E.F. (1964) 'Measuring the contribution of education', in *The Residual Factor and Economic Growth*, 13–55 and 77–102, Paris: OECD.

Denison, E.F. (1967) *Why Growth Rates Differ*, Washington: Brookings Institute.

Diamond, P. (1984) *A Search Equilibrium Approach to the Micro Foundations of Macroeconomics*, Cambridge, Mass.: MIT Press.

Doeringer, P.B. and Piore, M.J. (1971) *Internal Labour Markets and Manpower Analysis*, Lexington: Heath.

Dunlop, J.T. (1966) 'Job vacancy measure and economic analysis', in *The Measurement and Interpretation of Job Vacancies: A Conference Report*, New York: National Bureau for Economic Research.

Dutton, P.A. (1986) *The Impact of YTS on Engineering Apprenticeship: A Local Labour Market Study*, Research Report, Coventry: Institute for Employment Research, University of Warwick.

Ehrenberg, R.G. (1972) *Fringe Benefits and Overtime Behaviour*, Massachusetts: Lexington Books.

Elbaum, B. and Wilkinson, F. (1979) 'Industrial relations and uneven development: a comparative study of the British and American steel industries'. *Cambridge Journal of Economics* 3: 275–303.

Engineering Industry Training Board (1972) *The Costs of Training: A Preliminary Report*, Occasional Paper No. 2, Watford: EITB.

Engineering Industry Training Board (1975) *The Costs of Training Technicians and Technician Engineers*, Working Paper No. 1/1975, Research Planning and Statistics Division, Watford: EITB.

EITB/MSC (1986) *Careers of Young Women Technicians: Report of Studies of the Progress of Young Women Technicians Recruited Under the EITB Scholarship and Grant Schemes*, Occasional Paper No. 15, Watford: Engineering Industry Training Board.

European Commission (1981a) *Note on Wages and Incomes*, Rapid Information Note, No. 1–1981.

European Commission (1981b) *Labour Costs in 1978: Principal Results*, Luxembourg: SOEC.

Finniston, Sir M. (1980) *Engineering Our Future*, Report of a Committee Appointed by the Council for Scientific and Industrial Research, London: HMSO.

Fisher and Temin (1973) 'Returns to scale in research and development: what does the Schumpeterian hypothesis imply?', *Journal of Political Economy* 81: 56–70.

Fleming, M.C. (1970) 'Inter-firm differences in productivity and their relation to occupational structure and size of firm', *The Manchester School*, September, 223–45.

Food and Drink Manufacturing EDC (1983) *Review of the Food and Drink Manufacturing Industry*, London: National Economic Development Office.

Freeman, C. (1982) *The Economics of Industrial Innovation*, 2nd edn, London: Frances Pinter.

Freeman, R.B. and Medoff, J.L. (1979) 'The two faces of unionism', *The Public Interest* 57, Fall: 69–93.

Frenkel, S.J. (1986) 'The Australian Metal Workers Union and technological change: from collective bargaining to a labour market offensive', paper presented to Group C: Skills, Labour Markets, and Union Strategy, *Trade Unions, New Technology and Industrial Democracy Colloquium*, 6–8 June, Coventry: University of Warwick.

Griliches, Z. (1960a) 'Hybrid corn and the economics of innovation', *Science*, 29 July: 275–80.

Griliches, Z. (1960b) 'Measuring inputs into agriculture: a critical survey', *Journal of Farm Economics* 17(5): 1411–27.

Griliches, Z. (1970) 'Notes on the role of education in production functions and growth accounting', in Lee Hansen, W. (ed.), *Education, Income, and Human Capital*, Studies in Income and Wealth, 35: 71–115, National Bureau of Economic Research, New York: Columbia University Press.

Hakim, C. (1985) *Employers' Use of Outwork*, Research Paper No. 44, London: Department of Employment.

Hart, R.A. and Sharot, R. (1978) 'The short-run demand for workers and hours: a recursive model', *Review of Economic Studies* 45: 299–309.

Holt, C.C. (1971) 'Job search, Phillips' wage relations and union influence: theory and evidence', in Phelps, E.S. *et al.* (eds),

Microeconomic Foundations of Employment and Inflation Theory, London: Macmillan.

Holt, C.C. and David, M.H. (1966) 'The concept of job vacancies in a dynamic theory of demand for labour', *The Measurement and Interpretation of Job Vacancies*, Washington D.C.: National Bureau for Economic Research.

Hunter, L.C. *et al.* (1970) *Labour Problems of Technological Change*, London: George Allen and Unwin.

Industrial Society (1985) *Survey of Training Costs*, New Series No. 1, London: Industrial Society.

James, B. (1983) 'The trade union response to new technology', in Bosworth, D.L. (ed.), *Employment Consequences of Technological Change*, London: Macmillan.

Johansson, B. and Karlsson, C. (1985) 'Industrial applications of information technology: speed of introduction and labour force competence', Working Paper 1985, 4, CERUM, Umea: Umea University.

Kaldor, N. (1966) *Causes of the Slow Rate of Economic Growth in the United Kingdom*, Cambridge: Cambridge University Press.

Kaspura and Ho-Trieu (1980) 'Productivity and technological change in Australian 3-digit manufacturing industries 1968–9 to 1977–8', Department of Productivity Research Branch, Working Paper No. 10, Canberra.

Kendrick, J.W. (1961) *Productivity Trends in the United States*, Princeton: Princeton University Press.

Kendrick, J.W. and Grossman, E. (1980) *Productivity in the United States*, Baltimore: John Hopkins University Press.

Lawrence, P. (1984) 'Culture and ingenuity', *Human and Environmental Sciences Bulletin*, Loughborough: Loughborough University.

Lazonick, W.H. (1979) 'Industrial relations and technical change: the case of the self-acting mule', *Cambridge Journal of Economics* 3: 231–62.

Levinson, H.M. *et al.* (1971) *Collective Bargaining and Technological Change in American Transportation*, Evanston: Northwestern University.

Melman, S. (1956) *Dynamic Factors in Industrial Productivity*, Oxford: Basil Blackwell.

Metcalf, J.S. and Hall, P.H. (1983) 'The Verdoorn law and the Salter mechanism: a note on Australian manufacturing industry', *Australian Papers*, December.

Nasbeth, L. and Ray, G.F. (1974) *The Diffusion of New Industrial Processes: An International Study*, Cambridge: Cambridge University Press.

Nelson, R.R. (1981) 'Research on productivity growth: dead ends and new departures', *Journal of Economic Literature* 19 (3): 1029–64.

Nelson, R. and Winter, S.G. (1978) 'Forces generating and limiting concentration under Schumpeterian competition', *Bell Journal of Economics* 9: 524–48.

Northcott, J. and Rogers, P. (1982) *Microelectronics in Industry: What's Happening in Britain*, London: Policy Studies Institute.

Northcott, J., Rogers, P., Knetsch, W., and de Lestapis, B. (1985) *Microelectronics Industry – An International Comparison: Britain, Germany, France*, No. 635, London: Policy Studies Institute.

Pavitt and Soete (1980) 'Innovative activites and export shares: comparison between industries and countries', in Pavitt, K. (ed.), *Technical Innovation and British Economic Performance*, London: Macmillan.

Phelps, E.S. *et al.* (1971) (eds) *Microeconomic Foundations of Employment and Inflation Theory*, London: Macmillan.

Prais, S.J. (1981) 'Vocational qualifications of the labour force in Britain and Germany', *National Institute Economic Review* 98, November, 47–59.

Prais, S.J. and Wagner, K. (1983) 'Some practical aspects of human capital investment: training standards in five occupations in Britain and Germany', *National Institute Economic Review*, 105, August, 46–65.

Rainbird, H. and Grant, W. (1985) *Employers' Associations and Training Policy*, Research Report, Coventry: Institute for Employment Research, Warwick University.

Research Associates and Inbucon Management Consultants (1984) *The SEFIS 1 Scheme*, Report to the Department of Industry, London.

Schmookler, J. (1952) 'The changing efficiency of the American economy, 1869–1938', *Review of Economics and Statistics* 34(3): 214–31.

Schultz, T.W. (1960) 'Capital formation by education', *Journal of Political Economy*, 1960: 571–83.

Schultz, T.W. (1961) 'Education and economic growth', in Henry, N.B. (ed.), *Social Forces and Influences on American Education*, Chicago: Chicago University Press.

Schultz, T.W. (1963) *The Economic Value of Education*, New York.

Slichter, S.H. *et al.* (1960) *The Impact of Collective Bargaining on Management*, Washington: Brookings Institute.

Smith, A.D., Hitchens, D.M.W.N., and Davies, S.W. (1982) *International Industrial Productivity: A Comparison of Britain, America and Germany*, NIESR Occasional Paper, Cambridge: Cambridge University Press.

Solo, R. (1966) 'The capacity to assimilate an advanced technology', *American Economic Review, Papers and Proceedings*, May 91-7, reprinted in Rosenberg, N. (ed.) (1971), *The Economics of Technological Change*, 480–92, Harmondsworth: Penguin.

Solow, R.M. (1957) 'Technical change and the aggregate production function', *Review of Economics and Statistics* 39(3): 312–20.

Stoneman, P. (1984) 'An analytical framework for and an economic perspective on the impact of information technologies', paper presented to the DSTI/ICCP workshop, 27–28 June, Paris: OECD.

Tangri, O.P. (1966) 'Omissions in the treatment of the law of the variable proportions', *American Economic Review* June, 484–92.

Training Services Agency (undated) *Technicians: A Possible Basis for a TSA Programme*, Discussion Document, Sheffield: MSC.

Transport and General Workers Union (1978) *Microelectronics: New Technology/Old Problems/New Opportunities*, London: TGWU.

TUC (1979) *Employment and Technology*, London: TUC.

Wabe, S.J. (1974) 'Output and employment', in Wabe, S.J. *et al.*, *Manpower Forecasting for the Engineering Industry*, Research report No. 4, Watford: Engineering Industry Training Board.

Wabe, S.J. and Leech, D. (1978) 'Relative earnings in UK manufacturing – a reconsideration of the evidence', *Economic Journal* 88 (350): 296–315.

Whitehead, A.K. and Baruch, L. (1981) *People and Employment*, London: Butterworths.

Whitley, J.D. and Wilson, R.A. (1986) *Information Technology and Employment: Quantifying the Impact Using a Macroeconomic Model*, Research Report, Coventry: Institute for Employment Research, University of Warwick.

Williamson, O.E. (1967) 'Hierarchical control and optimal firm size', *Journal of Political Economy* 75: 123–38.

Wilson, R.A. (1984) *The Impact of Information Technology on the Engineering Industry*, Research Report, Coventry: Institute for Employment Research, University of Warwick.

Wilson, R.A. and Bosworth, D.L. (1986) *New Forms and New Areas of Employment Growth*, Draft Final Report of the UK Study, Report to the European Commission, Study No. 85397.

5

The Importance of Technology Transfer

Roy Rothwell and Mark Beesley

SMALL MANUFACTURING FIRMS (SMFs), INNOVATION, AND EXTERNAL TECHNOLOGY

Essentially we shall attempt to answer the question: 'Is lack of access to external technological know-how and expertise a barrier to growth in SMFs that have growth potential?'

Implicit in the question is the assumption that technological innovation is an important factor contributing to SMF growth. There exists convincing evidence, mainly from the United States, in support of this contention.[1] The US, however, appears to be a special case, since it is only there that new technology-based firms in *appreciable* numbers have grown rapidly to national and international importance. The factors underlying this phenomenon are: US post-war technological leadership; the entrepreneurial propensities of US technologists and academics; a large, dynamic, and innovation-demanding home market; the mobility of key individuals; relatively high availability of venture capital; and the very considerable R&D funding and procurement activities of the DoD and NASA. The high growth new technology-based firms (NTBFs) were associated mainly with emerging technologies in which the US enjoyed a leadership position, e.g. semiconductors, CAD and microcomputers. More recently NTBFs – mainly university spin-offs – have played a decisive role in the emergence in the US of the 'new wave' biotechnology industry.

Given that technological dynamism is a crucial factor in SMF growth, there is ample evidence to demonstrate that effective communication with external sources of scientific and technological expertise and advice is an important feature of successfully innovative firms. Lack of access to external know-how might, therefore, be considered as a barrier to innovation and hence to growth. The essential question then becomes: 'Are SMFs in the UK especially disadvantaged with respect to access to external technological know-how?'

There are two important aspects to this issue: *if* access to external technology is a barrier to innovation and growth in SMFs, is this because of infrastructural deficiencies (e.g. unfavourable attitudes on the part of universities, research associations and governmental laboratories; lack of information regarding sources of S&T expertise; the prohibitively high cost of external consultancies)? Or is it the result of deficiencies within the firms themselves (e.g. lack of in-house technical skills; lack of financial resources; lack of management time; inward-lookingness)?

In an attempt to answer these questions we will draw on the published literature, on our own researches at SPRU, on the experiences of professionals pursuing SMF research and on those of consultants actively involved with technology transfer to SMFs in the UK.

Appendix 5.1 (p. 100) lists the advantages and disadvantages generally ascribed to large and small firms in innovation which suggests, a priori, that comparative advantage in innovation is unequivocally associated with neither large nor small scale (Rothwell and Zegveld 1985). From the point of view of this paper, the two most pertinent statements are:

(i) 'SMFs often lack the time or resources to identify and use important external sources of scientific expertise and advice.'
(ii) 'SMFs often lack suitably qualified technical specialists. They are often unable to support a formal R&D effort on an appreciable scale.'

As we will demonstrate below, (i) and (ii) are interrelated.

Data – taken from the SPRU innovation data base – on the sources of major technological knowledge inputs to some 2,200 *important* innovations introduced by British companies between 1949 and 1979, throw some light on the first of the above two points (Rothwell 1986). Table 5.1 shows for small firms (employment less than 200) the percentages of innovatory ideas deriving from internal and external sources for the periods 1945–69 and 1970–9.

It can be seen that, during the period 1970–9, small firms gained nearly twice the percentage of technological innovation-

Table 5.1: Source of major innovation-initiating knowledge inputs to small-firm innovations in the UK

	1949–69	1970–9
In-house	83%	68%
External	17%	32%
% of innovations	14.8	19.5

initiating ideas from external sources than during the previous period. At the same time, small firms' share in total innovations increased to 19.5 per cent. A subsequent extension of the innovation data base to the period 1980–3 showed a further increase in small firms' innovation share to 26.3 per cent (Townsend *et al.* 1983). On the basis of these data it can be concluded that since 1970 small UK firms increasingly have been successful in accessing external technology and that their contribution to national manufacturing innovations has also increased.

The results of a recent SPRU questionnaire on the external linkages of 103 innovative SMFs in the UK confirm the external orientation of these firms (Beesley and Rothwell 1986). The questionnaire was distributed to SMFs contained in the SPRU innovation data base, all of which had contributed important innovations to the UK economy since 1945. The questionnaire, which was cross-sectoral, showed that: 39 per cent of firms subcontracted out a portion of their R&D; 26 per cent engaged in some form of collaborative R&D venture with other firms; 55 per cent enjoyed regular contacts with R&D activities being carried out in public sector institutes; 51 per cent enjoyed useful technical inputs from public sector institutes; and 40 per cent of firms had taken up at least one government-funded technology transfer/innovation assistance scheme.

A study undertaken in 1981 by CURDS (Newcastle University), into the local agglomeration economies used by a sample of innovative scientific instrument firms in Silicon Valley, Scotland and South East of England, also indicated high levels of external technological usage by innovative SMFs in the UK (Oakey 1984). Survey firms were asked if they maintained any external contact with sources of technical information of importance to in-house product and process developments. Perhaps surprisingly, the US firms recorded the lowest level of external R&D links (23 per

89

cent) compared with 56 per cent in Scotland and 42.4 per cent in the South East. Only a very small minority of the firms which used external technical links said that the breaking of the link would cause *serious* disruption to their innovatory performance (7 per cent in the South East; 11 per cent in Scotland; 5 per cent in Silicon Valley). According to the author of the study, the firms, and especially those located in Silicon Valley, were state-of-the-art leaders in technological development within their narrow product/market niches. The external technology utilized was seen as a complement to the firm's indigenous R&D activities and never as a substitute for them.

Significantly, it was in Scotland, where the rate of new product innovation was the lowest of the three regions, that shortages of R&D personnel constituted the main category of personnel shortage reported, representing 40 per cent of total shortages against 6.1 per cent in the South East and 11.1 per cent in Silicon Valley. It seems reasonable to suggest that there was greater pressure on firms in Scotland to complement in-house R&D expertise with external sources, which would at least partially account for the higher level (56 per cent) of Scottish firms utilizing external technological information. There was no indication in the study that firms wishing to gain access to external technology suffered severe problems in doing so.

An on-going ESRC-funded SPRU/Heriot-Watt study on regional entrepreneurship, local resource utilization and innovation in the South East, Scotland and Silicon Valley, which is a follow-up to the study reported above and which involves the same set of firms, yielded the following data on external technical contacts: South East, 50 per cent; Scotland, 26 per cent; Silicon Valley, 35 per cent. A number of the Scottish firms, whose external linkages had lapsed, claimed that they were now technological leaders in their particular niches and consequently no longer required external technological inputs. The impression gained was that there had been considerable know-how accumulation internally.

Twenty-seven per cent of firms in the South East and 12 per cent in Scotland stated that breaking the link would cause serious disruption to their innovatory performance. It seems that not only have more of the firms in the South East accessed external technology during the last five years, but also that it has become increasingly important to a larger proportion of them. As with the earlier study, however, gaining access to external technology was *not* perceived as an important problem.

Returning to point (ii) on p. 88, there exists evidence to suggest that shortages of technically skilled manpower can impede innovation and growth in small firms (CBI 1979; Walsh *et al.* 1980; Rothwell 1979; Oppenlander 1976). It was for this reason that the West German government introduced, in 1979, a scheme to subsidize the costs of R&D personnel in SMFs. An important aspect of employing in-house R&D professionals is the role they play in linking the firm to external sources of technology.

An evaluation of the West German SMF R&D personnel subsidy scheme yielded information on external technical linkages relevant to this enquiry:[2]

(i) More than 50 per cent of firms experienced no, or only minor, problems in gathering information about available technical solutions or in finding suitable technical consultants; only 6 per cent suffered severe problems.

(ii) Acquisition of information about *longer-term* technical trends presented problems to 20 per cent of firms, but 40 per cent claimed to have experienced no problems in this respect. However, more than 50 per cent of the companies surveyed claimed that it had not been necessary for them to seek such information during the preceding three years; of those that had, 50 per cent had experienced no information-gathering problems, 23 per cent claimed that insufficient information was available, and 22 per cent claimed that mounting a systematic search required the commitment of too much effort.

(iii) Fifty-eight per cent of the survey companies had co-operated with R&D institutes during the previous three years. Of the 42 per cent of companies that had not co-operated, 57 per cent claimed they were able satisfactorily to solve technical problems on the basis of in-house expertise.

Twenty-five per cent of all R&D personnel in the survey firms were professional scientists and engineers. The larger the size of one SMF, the more likely it was to employ graduates. However, since the economic performance of the survey firms was not systematically biased towards bigger companies, it was concluded that while employing graduates did facilitate the acquisition of new technology, they were not necessarily essential. (It should be borne in mind, however, that West German companies generally employ greater numbers of intermediate level technical personnel (technicians) than do their British counterparts.)

The importance to external technical communication of employing QSE was emphasized in a report published by the UK Universities and Industry Joint Committee in 1970 (CBI 1970). This showed that while small firms had fewer contacts with universities than their larger counterparts, a higher proportion of trained scientists in the senior management of small companies meant a greater likelihood of contact with universities.

Support for the view that employing graduates in a firm is important to establishing links with academics is provided by the results of a study undertaken by the Technical Change Centre (Angell *et al.* 1984). TCC surveyed the information-seeking behaviour of some 1,700 industrial scientists and engineers in Britain. Thirty-eight per cent of all respondents claimed to have regular contact with academics: the probability of having an academic contact was largely independent of firm size for firms employing up to 10,000. The point is, by definition, *all* the firms in the sample, both large and small, employed graduates.

The SPRU linkages study mentioned earlier (Beesley and Rothwell 1986) yielded additional supportive evidence. It showed that, in general, the volume of SMFs' external technical contacts increased with employment of R&D personnel. It is interesting, however, that a relatively high percentage of firms employing no full-time R&D staff did successfully access Department of Trade and Industry schemes; the figure increased only slightly with increasing R&D employment. Most of the DTI schemes taken up did, however, involve the use of technical consultants to transfer well-proven technology and related techniques which, even with relatively sparse in-house technical resources firms could readily assimilate. The same category of firms similarly effectively utilized the services of research associations whose technical activity might, perhaps, be assumed to focus largely on the solution of industry-wide, process-related problems and problems of standards, testing, and validation, rather than on new-product developments which might require complementary in-house technical resources.

If we are here considering barriers to growth in small firms *that have growth potential*, and especially technology-based small firms, then almost by definition they will employ qualified scientists and/or engineers capable of forging external technological linkages.

An important means by which firms can access external technological expertise is through the use of licensing. Data on licensing are generally sparse and unreliable, but a recent study by Lowe and Crawford investigated the factors influencing the use of licensing by British SMFs (Lowe and Crawford 1984). Lowe and Crawford estimate that only between 5 and 9 per cent of all SMFs engaged in licensing agreements (this includes licensing *in* and *out*). (In the recent SPRU questionnaire survey of external linkages by *innovative* small firms, 16 per cent of the firms licensed *in* products for manufacture.) In addition, licensing activity was clearly related to firm size – the smaller the firm, the less likely it was to engage in licensing activity. To a large extent this was because of organizational constraints within the smaller firms, in particular the high management-opportunity costs of finding and negotiating a licence. Another factor in successful licensing activity relates to the employment of qualified staff, with 96 per cent of the non-licensing firms not employing staff with either MSc or PhD qualifications.

According to Lowe and Crawford, although the means of entering licensing agreements is often *ad hoc* (informal meetings at conferences and exhibitions, for example), there exists a large number of licensing consultants and publications relating to licensing opportunities, able to provide systematic information and guidance. The authors conclude that: 'In general our research suggests that although there are major problems for smaller firms in utilizing licensing, *these can be overcome* and that licensing is a skill which can be learned even by firms without major resources' (p. 179).

A recent survey of technology strategies in 703 British companies of all sizes and in eight industrial sectors showed that, during the past ten years, 24.6 per cent of firms had licensed-in technology (which was only one of a large number of technology-acquisition techniques used) (BASE International 1986). A more detailed survey of 174 of the above companies showed that:

(i) Sixty-four per cent had acquired technology from sources outside their own group.

(ii) The intensity of using various methods of technology acquisition (and exploitation) was directly related to the size of the company's annual sales turnover.

(iii) Companies with low R&D expenditure (as a percentage of turnover) are less likely to be involved in exploiting their technology and are also less likely to be involved in the market for acquiring technology.

(iv) Twenty-nine per cent of firms experienced no major problems during technology deals involving the acquisition of technology. The problems that were experienced during technology acquisition were: negotiations too complex or too lengthy (22 per cent); inadequate finance (13 per cent); lack of knowledge or suitable personnel (17 per cent); disagreement over the technology to be included in the deal (16 per cent); disagreement over technology ownership (9 per cent); disagreement over the costs of acquiring the technology (29 per cent).

(v) Eighty-four per cent of firms acquiring technology expressed general satisfaction; two-thirds of these intended to acquire more technology in the future than they had in the past.

Twenty-two per cent of firms in the West German survey, discussed on page 91, had licensed-in technology during the last three years. This percentage increased with increasing firm size. It was also higher the higher the technological level of internal R&D. The more expansive the firm's corporate strategy, the more likely it was to license-in technology. Barriers to licensing-in were largely *internal* ones, such as lack of in-house expertise and experience and the 'not-invented-here' syndrome.

In summary, the evidence presented above suggests:

(i) During the 1970s, innovative small UK firms increasingly accessed external technology as an important input to their innovatory developments.

(ii) Innovative small UK firms enjoy high levels of R&D linkages with other companies and with infrastructural institutions. Their take-up of governmental S&T schemes is high.

(iii) Innovative small firms employ external technology as a complement to, and not as a substitute for, in-house R&D activities.

(iv) The employment of QSE in-house is an important enabling factor in accessing external technology.

(v) Small UK firms have made a growing contribution to national rates of innovation.

(vi) The ability of SMFs to license-in technology depends more on internal factors (skills, experience, resources) than on external ones (lack of sources or advice).

BARRIERS TO GROWTH: SOME EVIDENCE

In this section, the results of discussions with a number of British and foreign SMF experts and consultants on the factors influencing small-firm growth in general, and the role of access to external technology in particular, will be reported (see Appendix 5.2, p. 103). We begin by reporting the results of a recent meeting of the IRDAC Committee of the EC, which met to discuss, amongst other things, the problems faced by thirty innovative SMFs from seven European countries (including six from the UK) which were highly R&D-intensive and technological leaders in their particular fields (i.e. firms all having considerable growth potential).

The problems identified as being of most concern to the SMF managers were:

(i) *The need for more management training:* growth potential firms can experience considerable growth-related management problems especially when undergoing the 'entrepreneurial' to 'managed' transition.

(ii) *Skill shortages:* there was, in particular, a shortage of electronics skills.

(iii) *Forming partnerships:* SMFs experience difficulties in identifying suitable partners abroad.

(iv) *Finance:* access to start-up or 'seed' capital and capital to fund manufacturing start-up can be a problem.

(v) *Marketing:* all the firms were highly export oriented and often experienced difficulty in market start-up in the United States. More US market information would be an asset.

(vi) *Technical:* there was need for more R&D cash support for SMFs, especially to fund longer-term research. Better information on R&D centres throughout Europe would be helpful.

Access to external technology was *not* reported as a significant problem. Discussions with experts from West Germany, the Netherlands, Italy and the UK confirmed this point. The two most crucial factors in this respect were the willingness of the firm actively to seek external technology and the level of in-house skills (both technical and management) available to enable it effectively to assimilate and further develop externally acquired technology.

A recent (confidential) survey of thirty-three 'traditional' small firms in a variety of sectors, all located in Sussex, identified a number of barriers to growth. Among the most important barriers identified were:

(i) Lack of skilled labour and middle-management talent to support expansion.

(ii) Firms too 'comfortable' in their own particular niche.

(iii) Perceived problems in defending intellectual property rights with products having high market potential that might be of interest to a large corporation.

(iv) Lack of qualified staff to cope with the transition from a low-technology to a higher-technology level. Fear of losing qualified staff due to insufficient volume of interesting high-technology work.

(v) Managing the conflict between introducing new products and maintaining existing ones.

(vi) In the largely traditional firms interviewed, there was a lack of professional management and technical infrastructure. The usually 'qualified' MD is overburdened: he cannot push the technology down to lower levels in the firm. While access to technology is not a significant problem, *assimilating* new technology is a major growth-inhibitor.

According to BASE International, a UK business and technical consultancy firm intimately involved in the small-firms sector, the most important barriers to innovation and growth in SMFs are:

(i) Lack of management time to consider any business development activity.

(ii) Lack of vision and flair in the management team to consider the development of any new business areas beyond the existing experience.

(iii) Lack of resources, both financial and people, to implement any innovation strategy even if they had one.

In the opinion of Segal, Quince, and Wicksted (the UK economic and management consultants, and authors of *The Cambridge Phenomenon*), access to external technological know-how and advice is definitely *not* a barrier to growth in either traditional or technology-based SMFs wishing to develop, improve, and extend existing products and product ranges. Nor is access to new technology as a basis for major new product development for growth an important problem for SMFs. In the latter case the major constraint is the strategic perceptions and abilities of management, not identification of or access to technology *per se*. In the great majority of cases the employment of QSEs is essential for facilitating both SMFs' external contacts and for the assimilation of new technology.

According to Dr J.E. Aubert, a leading OECD expert on SMFs and innovation, small firms (both traditional ones and new technology-based ones) can gain access to all the standard technological know-how and advice that they need providing they have the desire and the will to do so. (Most European countries have well-developed technology assistance and information networks.) In the case of access to new technology for new applications, the answer is essentially the same, except perhaps in the case of acquiring information on very sophisticated new materials or components, which may be problematic. The employment of QSE is fundamental to SMFs' ability to identify and assimilate new technology.

The above views were confirmed in discussions with members of the Scottish Development Agency's Technology Transfer Division. While technology transfer is important to firms, and especially to the regeneration of existing firms, access was not the problem. The main problem areas are the commitment of management to seek, acquire, and assimilate external technology and their ability to integrate it into an overall business plan. In-house skills, both technological and management, and particularly strategic management skills, are essential to the efficient assimilation and proper utilization of external technology.

According to Dr Ron Loveland, Director of Wintech, those small firms which have growth potential already have the technology on board. The main problems they have are the financial resources to expand and the managerial skill to realize technological potential and growth. However, such firms are often not aware of technology from other areas which may help them, and Loveland feels that there is a role for intermediate agencies to bridge this information gap. But first of all it is necessary to make firms aware of the existence of a gap, and this often involves convincing senior management. As regards the importance of having skilled manpower within the firms in order to assimilate technology, while this is a problem area, Loveland regards it as less of a problem than getting managers to adopt a strategic approach to introducing new technology. Growth firms, by definition, are well 'plugged in' to external technology sources.

A comparative study of innovative SMFs in the UK (twenty-four firms) and West German (ten firms) metalworking and engineering sectors further underlined the importance of having an 'external orientation' and possessing in-house technical skills (Bessant and Grunt 1985). A fundamental characteristic of technical progressiveness in both countries was the willingness to take on external technology. While the general economic and financial environment was more favourable in West Germany, there was little difference with respect to external technological facilities: in both countries, SMFs could readily access external know-how provided they had the will to do so. There was a tendency for the West German firms to be more outward-looking than their British counterparts, which was associated with a higher incidence of technically qualified managers in Germany and a generally larger endowment of technically qualified personnel at all levels.

Finally, based on their survey of R&D performing SMFs in West Germany (see p. 91), and on the basis of extensive interviews with a wide variety of other West German SMFs, the ISI researchers have concluded that access to external technological expertise cannot be regarded as a barrier to growth in R&D performing SMFs.

CONCLUSIONS

We have been unable to obtain any evidence to suggest that lack of access to external technology and know-how is a significant barrier to growth in SMFs that have growth potential. Evidence presented here suggests that innovative SMFs in the UK generally enjoy high levels of external technical contacts both with other firms and with infrastructural institutions.

There was no evidence in the material surveyed to suggest that there are infrastructural deficiencies in the UK that particularly inhibit SMFs' access to external technology and technical expertise. The most important factors determining an SMF's propensity and ability to access external sources of technology are *internal* to the firm, most notably the employment of QSEs and the outward-lookingness of management.

The employment of QSEs is also an important determinant of an SMF's ability effectively to assimilate and exploit bought-in technology. Of perhaps even greater importance in this respect is the strategic ability of management to integrate externally acquired technology into an overall business plan.

While there exists evidence to suggest that small UK firms can experience major problems in licensing-in technology, these again are related primarily to internal rather than external factors. The most significant factors inhibiting small firms' licensing activities are management-opportunity costs (time and resources involved) and lack of in-house skills and expertise.

On the basis of our own research, our literature survey, and our discussions with SMF experts and consultants, we are led to the firm conclusion that assessing external technology and technical expertise does not, in general, present a significant problem to growth potential SMFs in the UK. (The same conclusion would appear to hold true for SMFs in other European advanced-market economies.) Problems which do occur in this respect arise, in the main, because of deficiencies within the SMFs themselves rather than as a result of deficiencies in the national S&T infrastructure.

Public policy initiatives that might go some way towards overcoming SMFs' internal deficiencies are:

(i) Subsidies to support the costs of employing technical specialists.

(ii) Training courses for SMF managers in the general area of technology strategy and management.

APPENDIX 5.1: ADVANTAGES AND DISADVANTAGES* OF SMALL AND LARGE FIRMS IN INNOVATION

	Small firms	Large firms
Marketing	Ability to react quickly to keep abreast of fast changing market requirements. (Market start-up abroad can be prohibitively costly.)	Comprehensive distribution and servicing facilities. High degree of market power with existing products.
Management	Lack of bureaucracy. Dynamic, entrepreneurial managers react quickly to take advantage of new opportunities and are willing to accept risk.	Professional managers able to control complex organizations and establish corporate strategies. (Can suffer an excess of bureaucracy. Often controlled by accountants who can be risk-averse. Managers can become mere 'administrators' who lack dynamism with respect to new long-term opportunities.)
Internal communication	Efficient and informal internal communication networks. Affords a fast response to internal problem solving; provides ability to reorganize rapidly to adapt to change in the external environment.	(Internal communications often cumbersome: this can lead to slow reaction to external threats and opportunities.)

	Small firms	Large firms
Qualified technical manpower	(Often lack suitably qualified technical specialists. Often unable to support a formal R&D effort on an appreciable scale.)	Ability to attract highly skilled technical specialists. Can support the establishment of a large R&D laboratory.
External communication	(Often lack the time or resources to identify and use important external sources of scientific and technological expertise.)	Able to 'plug-in' to external sources of scientific and technological expertise. Can afford library and information services. Can subcontract R&D to specialist centres of expertise. Can buy crucial technical information and technology.
Finance	(Can experience great difficulty in attracting capital, especially risk capital. Innovation can represent a disproportionately large financial risk. Inability to spread risk over a portfolio of projects.)	Ability to borrow on capital market. Ability to spread risk over a portfolio of projects. Better able to fund diversification into new technologies and new markets.
Economies of scale and the systems approach	(In some areas scale economies form substantial entry barrier to small firms. Inability to offer integrated product lines or systems.)	Ability to gain scale economies in R&D, production and marketing. Ability to offer a range of complementary products. Ability to bid for large turnkey projects.

	Small firms	Large firms
Growth	(Can experience difficulty in acquiring external capital necessary for rapid growth. Entrepreneurial managers sometimes unable to cope with increasingly complex organizations.)	Ability to finance expansion of production base. Ability to fund growth via diversification and acquisition.
Patents	(Can experience problems in coping with the patent system. Cannot afford time or costs involved in patent litigation.)	Ability to employ patent specialists. Can afford to litigate to defend patents against infringement.
Government regulations	(Often cannot cope with complex regulations. Unit costs of compliance for small firms often high.)	Ability to fund legal services to cope with complex regulatory requirements. Can spread regulatory costs. Able to fund R&D necessary for compliance.

* *Note*: The statements in brackets represent areas of potential *disadvantage*. Abstracted from Rothwell and Zegveld 1982.
Source: Rothwell & Zegveld 1985.

APPENDIX 5.2: SMF EXPERTS CONSULTED

Dr J.E. Aubert, DSTI, OECD, Paris, France.

Dr U. Kuntze, ISI Institute, Karlsruhe, West Germany.

BASE International, Milton Keynes, UK.

Scottish Development Agency, Technology Transfer Division, UK.

Dr R. Loveland, Director, Wintech, Welsh Development Agency, UK.

Dr F.-M. Kramer, Technical University, Berlin.

Segal, Quince and Wickstead, Cambridge, UK.

Dr H.A. Nicholls, Director, Aston Science Park, UK.

Mr Wim Vissers, Indivers Research, Netherlands.

Professor A. Gilardoni, University of Milan, Italy.

Mr H. Philips, Director, Pick-Up Scheme, University of Sussex, UK.

Dr R. Oakey, Heriot-Watt University, Edinburgh, UK.

Dr D. Storey, CURDS, University of Newcastle-upon-Tyne, UK.

NOTES

1. Evidence on the relationship between technological innovation and SMF growth is summarized in R. Rothwell and W. Zegveld (1982) *Innovation and the Small and Medium-Sized Firm*, London: Frances Pinter, Chapter 7: 'SMEs and employment'.
2. Personal communication from Dr Uwe Kuntze, ISI Institute, Karlsruhe. The evaluation results are claimed to be representative of 10,000 R&D performing West German SMFs.

REFERENCES

Angell, C.A. *et al.* (1984) *Information Transfer in Engineering and Science*, Research Report, London: Technical Change Centre.

BASE International (1986) *Technology Strategy and British Industry*, BASE Technology Report, Milton Keynes.

Beesley, M. and Rothwell, R. (1986) 'Small firms, intercompany linkages, and innovation', paper presented to the Ninth National Small Firms Policy and Research Conference, Gleneagles, Scotland, November (SPRU, University of Sussex Mimeo).

Bessant, J. and Grunt, M. (1985) *Management and Manufacturing Innovation in the United Kingdom and West Germany*, Aldershot: Gower.

CBI (1970) *Industry, Science, and the Universities*, Universities and Industry Joint Committee, July.

CBI (1979) *Growth in Manufacturing Industry*, London: CBI.

Lowe and Crawford (1984) *Innovation and Technology Transfer for the Growing Firm*, Oxford: Pergamon Press.

Oakey, R. (1984) *High-Technology Small Firms*, London: Frances Pinter.

Oppenlander, K.H. (1976) 'Das verhalten kleiner und mittlerer Unternehmen, in industriellen innovationz Prozess', in Oppenlander, K.H. (ed.), *Die Gesamt Wirtschaftliche Function Kleiner und Mittlerer Unternehmen*, Munchen: IFO Institute.

Rothwell, R. (1979) *Technical Change and Competitiveness in Agricultural Engineering: The Performance of the UK Industry*, SPRU Occasional Paper, Series No. 9, July.

Rothwell, R. (1986) 'Innovation and the smaller firm', in Brown, W. and Rothwell, R. (eds), *Entrepreneurship and Technology: World Practices and Experiences*, London: Longman.

Rothwell, R. and Zegveld, W. (1985) *Reindustrialization and Technology*, London: Longman.

Townsend, J. *et al.* (1983) *Science and Technology Indicators for the UK: Innovations in Britain since 1945*, SPRU Occasional Paper, Series No. 16, Science Policy Research Unit, University of Sussex.

Walsh, V.M. *et al.* (1980) *Technical Change and Skilled Manpower Needs in the Plastics Processing Industry*, SPRU Occasional Paper, Series No. 11, September.

6

Large Purchasers

Keith Hartley and John Hutton

In this study, large purchasers are defined to embrace both public- and private-sector bodies. Purchasing or procurement is defined narrowly to involve the acquisition of goods and services only, whilst generally excluding wider policy aims (e.g. protection of a domestic industrial base, jobs, high technology, and the balance of payments). A variety of experience is reported with the procurement of defence and medical equipment providing interesting case studies involving high-technology industries.

Nine related themes are classified concerning: the economics of procurement; the case for small firms; the implications for industrial structure; the contribution of economic theory to policy; the opportunities for trading; the role of markets in information and knowledge; barriers to entry and growth; and actual policy in the UK and overseas. A list of references is provided and some supporting case study material is presented in the Appendix on p. 123. A literature search (see References, p. 126) confirms that this is a subject area where very little theoretical and empirical work has been undertaken, especially by economists. In the circumstances, we have approached our terms of reference starting from first principles.

THE ECONOMICS OF PROCUREMENT:
THE ROLE OF LARGE PURCHASERS

Large buyers exist in both the public and private sectors. In the public sector, central government (e.g. MoD, PSA), the NHS, local authorities and the public corporations all purchase goods and services from private industry in the UK and overseas. For

105

some products such as defence and health, government is a major buyer for the output of such UK industries as aerospace, electronics, ordnance, shipbuilding, pharmaceuticals and medical equipment. Similarly, the public corporations buy most of their goods and services from private industry, with purchases totalling almost £13,000 m in the period 1979–80. Public corporations are major purchasers of the output of the mining machinery, electrical machinery, power-generating, transmission and distribution equipment, and railway equipment industries (Harlow 1983). Large private-sector firms are also major buyers (e.g. Rover; BP; British Telecom; GEC; Marks & Spencer) and, in some cases such as telecommunications equipment, their purchases form a substantial proportion of an industry's output.

Large buyers in both the public and private sectors can use their power to specify a product, to choose a supplier and to determine the type of contract to be awarded (e.g. fixed price; cost-plus). They have the power to influence the size, structure, competitiveness and efficiency of an industry; its technical progress via product and performance specifications; the prices paid for goods and services and ultimately; profitability. Large buyers can favour domestic over foreign suppliers and they can determine entry and exit for an industry (Hartley and Tisdell 1981, ch. 14). There is some evidence suggesting that industries which purchase from a few concentrated suppliers, or sell to a few concentrated buyers, tend to be less profitable (*ceteris paribus*). In other words, the more commodities an industry buys and the less concentrated are the industries producing these commodities, the more profitable will be the industry (Martin 1983).

THE CASE FOR SMALL FIRMS

From the views of economists, policy-makers and both small and large companies, there is general agreement that small firms have a number of advantages:

(i) A willingness and ability to innovate. For example, the MoD view is that small firms add to the competitive process through their qualities of enterprise and willingness to innovate (Cmnd 9227-I, 1984, p. 17). It seems that small enterprises have a comparative advantage at the beginning of the product life-cycle where most innovation occurs (Rothwell and Zegveld 1981,

p. 179). However, it is not at all obvious how the government might spot the winners at this point!

(ii) Greater motivation and commitment, i.e. the drive and entrepreneurship of small firms.

(iii) A fast and flexible response.

(iv) The performance of specialist tasks, especially those requiring a high labour content. Small enterprises are also more able and likely to respond to individual consumer demands for quality, individuality, and greater variety (e.g. the revival of real ale).

(v) Keeping prime contractors aware of the latest technology. For example, in the defence field, since small firms are usually less dependent on defence contracts, their greater involvement in civil commercial markets can result in a 'cross fertilization' from civil to military technology.

(vi) Civil exploitation of defence R&D (spin-off). Small firms believe that prime defence contractors hoard valuable ideas which small firms could profitably exploit in civil markets. Here, it is suggested that prime contractors often lack mechanisms for identifying and licensing such ideas (Appendix 6.2, p. 124).

(vii) It is claimed that small firms provide the seedbed of new initiatives from which will emerge the successful industries of the future. However, data show many independent entrepreneurs willing to try something out of the ordinary with many failing in the attempt (Beesley and Hamilton 1984).

(viii) Job creation. In the defence sector, there is some tentative evidence that small firms acting as sub-contractors in high-technology defence markets created more new jobs than similar high-technology small firms specializing in civil markets (Forrester and West 1985, p. 17).

(ix) Greater competition. For instance, in defence it has been estimated that if some of the barriers to entry (see below) could be reduced, the number of small firms competing for defence contracts could be doubled (Forrester and West 1985, summary; HCP 399, 1986, p. 155).

To sum up, small enterprises are believed to have a number of advantages in the innovation process. They might have dynamic enterpreneurs willing to react quickly and flexibly to changing consumer demands and new opportunities for profits. In contrast, large firms might be characterized by bureaucratic inertia and internal communications problems. However, small firms are faced with a number of disadvantages in the innovation process. They might face constraints on funding and access to qualified scientists and engineers; they might be unable to obtain scale economies and they might find it costly to cope with government regulations (Rothwell and Zegveld 1981, p. 180).

SMALL FIRMS, INDUSTRY STRUCTURE, AND PERFORMANCE

An extension of the number of small firms competing in markets will affect the structure of an industry by increasing rivalry and competitiveness. They will provide a competitive stimulus to established monopolies and oligopolies. Through their enterprise and willingness to innovate, small firms will improve industry performance by adding to the dynamic nature of markets. In view of these potential social benefits, questions arise as to whether a public policy is required for small firms. Firm growth paths and industrial structures are the subject of detailed analysis in another paper (chapter 8). These issues are crucial to the determination of the effects of procurement policy on small firms.

DOES ECONOMIC ANALYSIS OFFER ANY GUIDELINES FOR A GOVERNMENT PROCUREMENT POLICY WHICH FAVOURS SMALL FIRMS?

Economic analysis suggests that if society favours a properly working market economy, then governments might intervene where private markets are not working correctly. Markets can fail because of major imperfections (e.g. monopoly, restrictive practices, entry barriers) or external effects (e.g. pollution). State intervention in favour of small firms might be justified where market failures operate so as to penalize small enterprises.

On a market failure view, government purchasing favouring small firms might be justified in the following situations:

(i) Where a market is dominated by monopoly or oligopoly and entry barriers.

(ii) Information failures, i.e. where markets are providing 'too little' information on trading opportunities in the economy. An obvious starting point is the public sector which, in principle, might be more easily required to change its behaviour.

(iii) Externalities, where private markets if left to themselves will provide too few small firms, i.e. fewer than society regards as desirable.

The market failure case for public procurement favouring small firms needs to be interpreted carefully. There is a danger that it will be used to justify any form of government intervention. Indeed, even if it is shown that there is a case for a public policy towards small enterprises, it does not follow that government purchasing is the only or the most appropriate form of intervention. Other policies such as advisory and technical assistance services, subsidies or training might be more appropriate.

Critics of a procurement policy favouring small firms will stress the extra costs involved in preferential purchasing which interferes with free trade within the economy. However, any extra costs might be offset by wider social benefits (e.g. dynamic markets; dispersion of economic and political power). Moreover, an official report identified a number of features of government procurement policy which were likely to penalize small firms (Cmnd 4811, 1971, p. 108):

(i) Competitive tenders are more often selective than open; and small firms might have difficulty in proving their competence for inclusion on an approved list. Similarly, a 1975 report on public purchasing from the construction industry favoured selective to open competition: 'there is merit in restricted lists predominantly of firms with a record of satisfactory work for the client . . . although such lists should not be exclusive of newcomers' (NEDO 1975, p. 45). Significantly, there was no reference to how newcomers might be encouraged!

(ii) Procurement officers are likely to prefer a large, established, well-known firm to an unknown smaller enterprise. Procurement officers seeking to avoid risks will be reluctant to award a contract to a new, unknown small contractor lacking an established reputation.

(iii) The trend towards larger-size contracts is excluding small firms. It has been suggested that this trend 'sometimes goes beyond the point of maximum economies of scale' (Cmnd 4811, 1971, p. 108). For these reasons, the report concluded that the growing importance of the public sector as a buyer of goods and services was likely to be detrimental to small firms: a conclusion

109

which reinforces the case for a policy emphasis on the public sector as a source of market failure.

An economics of politics approach provides an alternative explanation of why procurement policy might favour large rather than small firms. On this view, vote-seeking governments and budget-conscious bureaucracies are likely to award contracts to large firms which form clearly identifiable producer groups offering substantial benefits in the form of jobs, technology and balance of payments contributions to the UK economy (i.e. 'good value for money'). Contracts can be awarded to large firms in politically-sensitive locations; politicians and civil servants might enjoy the prestige of dealing with large contractors; and, on retirement, politicians and civil servants might be offered a seat on the board of a major contractor (Hartley and Tisdell 1981, chs 3, 14–15).

TRADING OPPORTUNITIES

In choosing whether to undertake work 'in-house' or to use outside suppliers, a profit-seeking firm will compare the relative costs, benefits (including risks) and ultimately profitability of the options. The choice between 'in-house' and 'buying-in' is similar to the situation facing nations in the world economy where they have to decide whether to support their domestic industry (e.g. nationalism, protection) or shop around and benefit from international trade based on comparative advantage. Similar choices are involved in the policy debate about competitive tendering for local authority and NHS services (Hartley and Huby 1985). Elsewhere, the industrial economics literature explains the existence of firms and the extent of their activities in terms of transaction costs (Williamson 1975).

In choosing between in-house and outside suppliers, there is substantial agreement between both large and small firms on their relative strengths. Large firms have advantages in large-scale investment, large production batches, the co-ordination and control of projects, risk-spreading and marketing (including lobbying). Small firms were believed to have relative advantages in motivation and commitment reflected in low costs for small quantities, flexibility, speed of response, innovation, and fast delivery.

Large firms face considerable pressures to keep work in-house, especially in periods of recession and uncertainty. In-house work protects a large firm's existing staff, including its trained labour. In effect, the costs of any variations in a large firm's workload can be shifted to outside suppliers. And the extent to which work is contracted-out determines the volume of business (size of market) available to small firms. Where small firms are allowed to bid against the in-house production of large firms, they are often able to compete successfully. In other words, there are opportunities for transferring work from the divisions of prime contractors to smaller firms in those activities where small firms as sub-contractors are more efficient (Forrester and West 1985, pp. 31–4). This apparent failure by firms to undertake an adequate market search and to exploit potentially profitable trading opportunities raises two questions:

(i) Why are large firms failing to exploit these opportunities? Possible explanations include a manager's concern with a quiet life and non-profit objectives which can be related to the degree of competition in product and capital markets, to the internal organization of firms (e.g. competing divisions) and to the nature of employment contracts in large firms (e.g. payment by age rather than performance). Alternatively, there might be major failures in information markets which governments might be able to correct at reasonable cost (e.g. via a public information and education service).

(ii) How large are the savings from competition and possible contracting-out of in-house activities? Evidence from the current public-sector competitive tendering initiatives suggests cost savings of some 25 per cent (Hartley and Huby 1985).

In the public sector, procurement is concerned with obtaining good value for money. A lengthy checklist of short-, medium-, and long-term considerations (including competition for future supplies) has been formulated, although no guidance has been given on how the various factors are to be measured and valued (*Government Purchasing* 1984, p. 47). In these circumstances, government procurement officers have considerable discretion in their interpretation of good value for money (e.g. a consideration of wider objectives such as jobs, technology, and the balance of payments). Purchasing departments often prefer stable relationships with suppliers whose reputation and quality are well known.

111

Changing suppliers at frequent intervals can be disruptive, inconvenient and not without cost (Harlow 1983, p. 44).

In defence, the introduction of a competitive procurement policy has extended trading opportunities. Between 1979 and 1986, the proportion of contracts let by competition and market forces increased from 30 per cent to 64 per cent and MoD has claimed average cost savings of over 30 per cent from introducing competition (Cmnd 9227-I, 1984, p. 17).

INFORMATION MARKETS

Trade, exchange, and the development of markets requires that buyers and sellers have access to information. Buyers have to search the market to identify and locate potential suppliers and then determine their reputation for reliability and quality. Similarly, suppliers seeking profitable opportunities have to identify the range of demands from public- and private-sector buyers and the relevant decision maker in the buying organization. Searching by buyers and sellers involves costs (including a learning process) and will be undertaken so long as it is expected to be worthwhile (Parkinson 1985).

The search process by buyers will depend upon the motivation of buyers, the incentives and rewards for good performance and the penalties for failure, all of which will affect their attitudes towards risk-taking. For example, the employment contracts of civil servants provide no incentives to economize in buying. Instead, there is every inducement to abide by the rules of 'public accountability' and to shift decision making to an amorphous committee, with the taxpayers and ratepayers bearing the financial consequences of mistakes (e.g. cost escalation, delays, gold plating).

Buyer confidence in the supplier is a major factor in selecting a supplier. Buyers seeking to avoid risks prefer to rely on established suppliers with an established reputation (i.e. tried and safe solutions). New suppliers are regarded as a major risk and success for a new entrant willl 'come from persistence and chance' (Forrester and West 1985, p. 12; p. 21). A study of machine tool purchases found that one-third of all purchases were determined on *one* quotation – sometimes more than one quotation was obtained (usually 2–3) to conform to company policy. Interestingly, buyers preferred purchases from suppliers of whom they had previous experience and this was especially the case for the very large purchasing companies (Cunningham and White 1974). Buyers also believe that the growth process for small firms represents a further risk factor. With growth, various crisis points are reached where existing management controls in the small firm cease to be adequate.

In the high-technology markets such as defence, buyers search for sub-contractors in a variety of ways:

(i) Document search, e.g. trade directories, journals, and specialist literature.

(ii) Trade sources, e.g. other major firms, trade associations.

(iii) In-house sources, e.g. experience, personal knowledge, previous bids.

Some evidence is available on the reasons why small high-technology firms do not enter certain markets. One survey found that amongst the major reasons for *not* entering the defence high-technology market were:

(i) No information on market opportunities.

(ii) Not knowing where to ask (this, of course, might be a reflection on the firm's lack of entrepreneurship).

(iii) A reluctance to become involved in complicated procedures and paperwork and the costs of approved quality standards.

ENTRY BARRIERS

Just as the existence of large suppliers in a market can create entry barriers to new firms, the presence of large purchasers can create similar problems for small firms. Of the conventional barriers to entry, lack of technical knowledge is unlikely to be serious for small firms, as they are often the innovators in high-technology industries. However, barriers to entry in the form of economies of scale and customer loyalty to existing products may be enhanced by the procurement policies adopted by large organizations in the public and private sectors. The beliefs of small firms might also deter entry.

Procurement decisions are influenced by a range of factors including supply price, after-sales service, product quality and specification, security of future supply and the attitudes of buyers (Felch 1985; McGoldrick and Douglas 1983). Supply price is likely to be a dominant consideration when buying a relatively homogeneous product from one of many potential suppliers. For specialized products, which are crucial to the purchaser's operations and are only obtainable from a limited number of sources, the emphasis is more likely to be on after-sales service and security of supply. In this case the purchaser has a direct interest in the survival of the supplier and may be less keen to drive down costs to the minimum. In markets dominated by large public-sector organizations, such as defence or medical equipment, the pursuit of apparently self-interested and cost-minimizing procurement policies may create or enhance entry barriers which are not inherent in the industry's cost and production characteristics (e.g. by reducing potential profitability and by favouring established suppliers).

The potential advantages of small firms wishing to enter a market often arise from: an innovative product or process which leads to increased effectiveness or lower cost of the product; flexibility of response in terms of meeting deadlines; and lower overheads than more established firms. A large purchaser with a *centralized procurement policy* can neutralize all these advantages by:

(i) Adopting conservative specifications which exclude truly innovative products, or by applying exhaustive product-testing requirements before adding firms to lists of approved suppliers. Often buyers are sensitive to risk, so that they prefer existing proven suppliers rather than incurring the costs and risks of 'doing business with strangers'.

(ii) Delaying decisions and affecting the viability of smaller firms waiting for business.

(iii) Requiring detailed tender submissions which stretch the resources of the smaller firm and push up the overhead costs.

In contrast, a *decentralized procurement policy*, with decision making by local managers, can be of great benefit to smaller suppliers. Individual contracts will be of a smaller size, so that reliability in supply can be demonstrated without the risks of taking on very large commitments at the outset (the risk to the purchaser is also less). The greater number of contracts will increase the likelihood of success for a particular firm. In sacrificing any cost-savings which might result from more exploitation of buying power, the decentralized organization facilitates the adoption of innovations which may be of greater long-term benefit to the organization, and which keep the structure of the supplying industry more fluid and dynamic (Cmnd 9867, 1986, p. 94).

Some evidence of the effect of procurement-related entry barriers is available from the defence and medical equipment sectors. One attitudinal survey found a series of factors deterring entry into the supply of defence equipment by small firms (apart from lack of knowledge of trading opportunities discussed in the previous sections). From the perspective and beliefs of small firms, these include:

(i) Fears of delays in payment by large customers with possible implications for the viability of small firms (Cmnd 9867, 1986, p. 94). Since MoD aims to pay its contractors within thirty days, it seems possible that larger firms are profiting at the small firm's expense; although this should make business with small companies more attractive!

(ii) The cost of tendering when there is uncertainty over the real chance of success.

(iii) The cost of convincing potential purchasers of the seriousness of their tenders and their ability to meet the conditions of contract. They have to create sufficient confidence in the buyer to be given a first chance. Small firms believe that they are only able to influence about half of the decision-making process whereby large buyers select suppliers (Forrester and West 1985, p. 25).

In some cases actually identifying the real decision maker in a large organization proved difficult for smaller firms without a large technical and marketing staff. The survey also found that large firms in high-technology defence markets did not operate a sub-contracting and purchasing policy which encouraged small firms. Many tender invitations were non-serious – merely to observe company requirements for a minimum number of bidders when the supplier had already been chosen on non-price factors. The cost of tender preparations and submission for small firms could represent 2.5 per cent to 3 per cent of the contract value, and if the number of genuinely 'open' contracts was believed to be limited, the reluctance of small firms to compete was understandable. Given the uncertainties which abound in such markets, the small firms which succeed are those which learn the fastest how to identify 'winnable' contracts. Often, however, chance would play a part as contracts open to new entrants usually arose when established suppliers failed or experienced unforeseen problems, or demand increased unexpectedly (Forrester and West 1985, pp. 21–2).

The UK medical equipment industry has a dominant public-sector purchaser in the NHS (although over 40 per cent of UK output in the industry is exported, and over 40 per cent of UK purchases are imported, ACARD 1986). The industry is characterized by a large number of relatively small suppliers in most sub-markets. Traditionally, a decentralized approach to equipment procurement has been adopted with considerable autonomy for individual regional and district health authorities, and strong influence exerted by equipment-users in procurement decisions (Hartley and Hutton 1982). In those areas where there has been the greatest amount of central co-ordination of purchasing (e.g. radiological equipment), the number of suppliers was lowest and the average firm size largest. A more recent example of the effects of centralized contracting acting as a barrier to new products and firms is the wheelchair and artificial-limb market. In this case it appeared that centralization did not even achieve cost savings or reliability of supply (DHSS 1986).

A survey of the UK medical equipment industry found a difference of opinion over the preferred direction of change in NHS procurement policy (Hartley and Hutton 1982). Small firms wished to see greater decentralization of decision making, and a reduction of the time taken to reach decisions in the complex series of committees. Larger firms with currently popular products wished to see more centralization. Many firms suggested a more positive approach to procurement to encourage new entry and product development. For instance, suggestions were made for the guaranteed purchase of a given number of a new product to reduce the risk for R&D investment. Of those firms supplying the NHS and private-sector customers, most found dealing with the latter more straightforward although tendering might be more rigorously used.

Governments can also extend market opportunities through their policies on competitive tendering and de-regulation. Such policy measures reduce barriers to entry. Competitive tendering requires public bodies such as the NHS and local authorities to invite competitive bids for activities which traditionally have been undertaken in-house (e.g. refuse collection; catering; cleaning of hospitals, offices and streets; local bus services: Kay *et al.* 1986). In this way, private firms of all sizes are able, in principle, to bid for business which used to be reserved for the in-house unit. Of course, small firms still have the problems and costs of gaining access to approved lists of contractors.

Some of the apparent entry barriers for small firms need to be interpreted carefully and critically. For example, supporters of small firms claim that non-serious tender invitations are a burden to small businesses and can create a misleading impression of the true volume of work available. However, such criticisms resemble a counsel of perfection and it is not obvious that there is a real economic problem (and if there is, what can be done about it). In an uncertain world, all tendering involves costs and risks and is part of the process of searching the market: firms will seek to recover their tendering costs over the long-run and they will soon learn about the buying policies of large firms and whether a contract is winnable (e.g. via contact with other small firms). Similarly, small firms often complain that they have never been asked to quote for public contracts. Such complaints might be partly a reflection on the firm's lack of enterprise and competitiveness and on its reluctance to search for business. At the same time, it is possible that relatively cheap improvements in communications, especially for public-sector buyers, might increase significantly the number of firms competing in markets.

BARRIERS TO GROWTH

The problems of breaking into a market are serious for small firms, but the maintenance or expansion of a market position may be equally difficult. The growth of small firms may be assisted or hindered by the procurement policies adopted by their large customers (Cmnd 9867, 1986, p. 94).

Ironically, the procurement policy which improves the chances of *entry* (i.e. decentralized decision making) may cause problems for small firms wishing to *expand*. If the separate units of a public-sector organization (e.g. the district health authorities), do not exchange information on suppliers, a firm successful with one public customer may have to repeat its marketing effort many times over in other places, even if the superiority of the product has been clearly shown. The cost of this will fall proportionately more heavily on a small firm. A centralized and co-ordinated register and information system could lead to a rapid build-up of demand for a successful firm, without the need for a centralized contracting system. This approach was introduced by the now defunct NHS Supply Council, and has been embraced by the new NHS Procurement Directorate (Critchley 1986).

Once a product's advantages are established, a public-sector user and supplier have a mutual interest in its diffusion until something better is developed. Whether the next innovation is more likely to come from a firm with a record of past successful innovation or from a new firm is uncertain. For example, DHSS policy on the procurement of pharmaceuticals favours existing firms by allowing research costs to be recouped in the pricing structure. This guarantees a continuous R&D effort by existing firms, which are relatively large, supported by a patent system which protects income arising from successful innovation (Maynard and Hartley 1984). Although the technical requirements of entry into the pharmaceutical market are likely to deter small firms, the procurement practices encourage the growth of existing suppliers and reinforce the entry barriers to newcomers.

The characteristic small producer of medical equipment was a feature of this industry highlighted by the recent ACARD study: 'the pattern we have discerned of a large number of "national niche producers" unable, and perhaps to some extent *unwilling* to break out of their niches and achieve growth' (ACARD 1986, para. 62, emphasis added). Decentralized procurement was cited as a prime factor in producing the industrial structure, although the motivation of small firms (their unwillingness to grow) cannot be ignored.

Further evidence of the potential for growth in the medical equipment industry was the fact that, on average, suppliers could have reduced unit costs by some 17 per cent if output levels were doubled (Hartley and Hutton 1982). This would undoubtedly have reduced the number of suppliers, but firms seemed reluctant to adopt an expansionist strategy by risking investment in more capacity and competing for market share on price. The current financial climate in the NHS and the increasing attention to cost-effectiveness in procurement may now make firm expansion a more attractive strategy, but unless the diverse preferences of clinical users of equipment can be standardized through more centralized procurement, this route to growth may still be very risky.

118

Defence procurement is also interesting since it involves high technology and a relatively small number of large prime contractors (e.g. British Aerospace, Rolls Royce, Royal Ordnance, GEC). The sub-contracting policies of the prime contractors can have a major impact on the profitability and growth of small firms. In general, MoD policy since 1983 has allocated more defence contracts to prime contractors, leaving the prime contractor (and not MoD) to select its sub-contractors. However, MoD expects prime contractors to use competition in selecting sub-contractors and in determining whether work should be undertaken in-house or by an outside contractor (Cmnd 9227-I, 1984, p. 17). Survey evidence suggests that small firms as sub-contractors are not obtaining open access to competition in areas where they are more efficient: hence MoD is not receiving value for money 'and small firms are not receiving the maximum boost to growth which would be justified from their performance capabilities' (Forrester and West 1985, summary). An alternative view has claimed that 'imposed competition at the sub-contract level forced firms to adopt demonstrably uncommercial policies' (PA 1986, p. 4).

PROCUREMENT POLICY IN THE UK AND OVERSEAS

UK policy

Economic theory suggests some possible guidelines for a public policy towards small firms. Also, for some time, it has been recognized that there is scope for the deliberate use of the government's purchasing power to support enterprise and innovation among small firms (Cmnd 4811, 1971, p. 107). The NEDC report on the UK information technology industry recommended that government procurement policy should be used to 'encourage competitive UK companies including smaller and non-traditional suppliers' (NEDC 1982, p. 28). However, the UK has no specific procurement policies favouring small enterprises.[1]

Current UK policy aims to give small firms improved access to government business: it does not favour small firms irrespective of their competitiveness (*Government Purchasing* 1984, p. 34). Instead, for small firms, some of the procedures for tendering have been simplified, and the DTI and some individual departments (e.g.

MoD, PSA) have produced booklets providing information on public purchasing (DTI 1985; MoD 1986). For defence work, small firms are advised to seek sub-contract business and MoD does not intervene directly in the relationship between prime and sub-contractors. However, as part of its competition policy, MoD is seeking to encourage competition at the sub-contract level, including competitive checks on a prime contractor's in-house facilities. But the Ministry lacks a systematic basis for the collection of statistics for competition at the sub-contract level (HCP 399, 1986, p. 155). Indeed, this lack of data raises a more general point. Policy-makers cannot operate without basic information. In this context, the government does not hold central records of how much of its business is awarded to small firms (*Government Purchasing* 1984, p. 34).

Current UK policy accepts that departments will incur a small cost in encouraging small firms to bid for government business. None the less, the policy is expected to be worthwhile, with the longer-term savings to departments outweighing the costs (*Government Purchasing* 1984, p. 35).

Overseas experience

A study of ten European nations found that data on the share of public contracts awarded to small firms were not available (EIU, 1983, p. 51).[2] Within Europe, few countries had specific procurement policies favouring small firms. West Germany had a government commitment to fair shares for small firms; whilst the French government gave small firms a second chance in matching the lowest bid from large firms if their initial tender was within 4 per cent of the large competitors. The report concluded by ranking the ten nations according to how their *broad* procurement policy favoured small enterprises. On this basis, West Germany and the Netherlands were the top-ranking nations (i.e. with procurement policies most favourable to small firms); whilst the UK was in a third group of nations alongside Denmark, Eire and Greece (EIU 1983, p. 83).

In the USA, Federal agencies are required to place a fair proportion of their total purchases with small businesses. In addition, during the 1960s and 1970s, the Buy American Act required the US government to favour US suppliers so long as their products were priced no more than 6 per cent higher than the lowest bidder offering foreign products. The prices used in these comparisons were delivered prices including duty and transport costs.[3] The preference was increased from 6 per cent to 12 per cent for bids from US small firms (OECD 1976, p. 127).

During the 1960s, the US Defense Department became concerned that small firms were not receiving their fair share of defence business. In particular, there were worries about the magnitude of non-competitive procurement of spare parts from original equipment manufacturers and efforts were made to introduce more competition for these purchases. It was found that US defence business was concentrated on the top twenty-five firms which received 45 per cent of the budget. Small firms were not receiving their fair share for two reasons:

(i) The multiplicity of codes and regulations which the government had created to guarantee product quality.

(ii) Compliance with these costly and complex measures discouraged many small firms from bidding for government contracts.

There was also buyer resistance to change. Department of Defense buyers had a low-risk attitude to purchasing spare parts so they preferred (especially when in doubt) buying spares from the original manufacturer. Efforts to increase competition for spare parts encountered two problems:

(i) Patents were held by the original manufacturer.

(ii) Entry to a restricted list of approved suppliers can be costly for small firms (Trinkous and Corrin 1984).

CONCLUSIONS

Procurement and small firms is an area where there are major gaps in our knowledge. For many of the issues outlined in the terms of reference, there was a general lack of published information and relevant studies. In some cases, the analytical framework (theory) needs further development (e.g. on the routes along which the relationships between large firms and their suppliers may develop over time as suppliers grow in size).

Given the general absence of data, a first requirement is to improve the available information. *Government could be required to publish an annual report showing the proportion of its business awarded to small firms.* Ideally, the information needs to be provided for each central government department, local authorities, the NHS, and the nationalized industries, and needs to be related to the supplier industries on the basis of the Standard Industrial Classification.

Further investigation is needed to assess the impact of current policy initiatives on small firms. For example: are public buyers reviewing approved lists, excluding poor performers, and inviting new applications? Do tender invitations include at least one firm which has not previously been invited to tender (*Government Purchasing* 1984, p. 11)? Questions also arise as to whether the current policy initiative has been successful: why have some small firms succeeded and others not? How did firms obtain information on government business and what difficulties did they encounter in gaining entry to an approved list? Answers to these questions require further research into the actual experience of both buyers and small firms in tendering for government contracts. Information is needed on the views both of small firms and public procurement officials on the following issues:

(i) What are the difficulties of obtaining information and access, e.g. what are the problems and costs to small firms of gaining entry to an approved list? How do small firms acquire information about government contracts?

(ii) What are the reasons for success and failure and what happens as small firms grow in size?

(iii) What is the experience of small firms on an approved list? For example: how often are they invited to tender? How successful are they and how do they react to an unsuccessful bid?

(iv) Does decentralized purchasing favour small enterprises?

Answers to these questions will provide the basis for assessing whether, for example, government purchasing policy should require a minimum proportion of contracts to be awarded to small firms.

In relation to purchasing, especially by public bodies, a number of major barriers to the growth of small firms have been identified:

(i) *Internal factors.* These include the *organization of buying* (centralization v decentralization) and the *incentive system for buyers* which affects their attitude to risk and their willingness to search the market. On the supply side, the *qualities of entrepreneurship* will determine a small firm's willingness to search for profitable opportunities.

(ii) *External factors* comprise the general category of market failures concerned with information and entry conditions.

APPENDIX 6.1
EXPERIENCE OF SMALL FIRMS: A CASE STUDY

Because of the lack of literature on the experiences of small firms in dealing with large purchasers, further information was sought from two large private companies and a small firm dealing with large purchasers from both the public and private sectors. Many of the issues raised in the main paper were brought out in these discussions. The main points were as follows:

(i) Large organizations have hierarchical procurement systems, with rules varying according to the scale of contract. In most cases discretionary purchases could be made by procurement staff, without tender competition, below a certain value.

(ii) An important consideration for large private companies was reliability and promptness of delivery of supplies, as their own customers expected deadlines to be met. Familiarity with a supplier could be more important than size in this context.

(iii) Large companies could be very conservative in their approach to innovative products. These were more likely to be accepted from established suppliers than new, small firms, regardless of apparent technical merit. One-off sales of specialist equipment were more likely to be achieved if the relevant engineering personnel, rather than procurement staff, controlled the procurement process.

(iv) From the perspective of the small firm, all large organizations (public or private) presented problems. Generally, open tendering was preferred as a way of entering a market as the small firm's price advantage could be exploited. Where selective tendering applied, problems were experienced in getting onto the approved list of suppliers. In discretionary purchases the small firm seemed to be least successful in gaining business.

(v) While preferring tender competition, the amount of documentation requested was a burden to smaller firms. There was no apparent difference between public and private negotiations in the scale of requirements which could vary from 160 to 30 pages (the largest and smallest were both private companies). Public-sector purchasers took longer to reach decisions on tenders, but all large organizations were slow payers.

APPENDIX 6.2
DEFENCE AND SPIN-OFF

The problem

Concern is often expressed that there is 'too little spin-off' from defence R&D to the civil sector. Large defence contractors have been criticized for hoarding or sitting on the results of defence R&D (CSS 1986, p. 41; Maddock 1983).

Causes of the problem

(i) Spin-off from defence R&D is an aspect of the market in ideas and how well the market works in transferring ideas from defence to the civil sector.

(ii) Markets in information, knowledge, and ideas are extremely complex, with agents seeking to establish intellectual property rights in their ideas. The hoarding or transmission of ideas will depend upon the behaviour of the various agents in the market: e.g. scientists who discover a new idea; the organization employing the scientist (e.g. government research establishment, university, company) and the incentives which exist for marketing ideas outside of their immediate defence context; the MoD which will be concerned about the national security aspects of defence R&D; the corporate sector which will have to sell any new product in civil markets; and financiers who have to supply the necessary funds.

(iii) If a lack of 'spin-off' is a problem, it suggests a failure by buyers and sellers to exploit commercially the available knowledge. Does civil industry know the possibilities and opportunities for using and applying defence R&D? How does it acquire information on the available opportunities and is it costly to find out? Similarly, how do defence R&D establishments seek commercial outlets for their military ideas?

(iv) It has been suggested that many small firms, who are often the main source of innovative developments, are unaware of information that defence R&D establishments have to offer. At the same time, small firms find it difficult to approach MoD (a psychological barrier) which they believe to be a monolithic, bureaucratic and highly-secret organization (MoD 1982, p. 3).

Policy solutions

(i) It is believed that the benefits from fall-out could be increased if there were machinery to ensure that potentially valuable research reached British firms who could make use of it. In this context, various proposals have been made for creating a scientific clearing house or technological broker or a data-information bank to promote the diffusion of ideas.

(ii) In late 1985, Defence Technology Enterprises Ltd (DTE) was created. DTE is the result of a joint initiative by MoD and a number of banks and finance houses which became DTE's founding shareholders. DTE aims to assist in the transfer of defence technology to the civil sector. Its staff have access to selected defence R&D establishments where they can identify technology with commercial potential, disseminate information about it to a wide range of companies and arrange to license the technology to entrepreneurs (MoD 1986). On this basis, DTE can be regarded as an agency to improve information flows and the transmission of ideas from defence R&D to the civil sector.

NOTES

1. As an example of the use of purchasing power, it is interesting to note that during its existence, the GLC required approved contractors to be equal opportunity employers; but small firms with under twenty people were not subject to the same detailed scrutiny as larger employers (Carr and Smith 1985).

2. Less than 4 per cent of the study was devoted to public procurement.

3. In 1962, as an interim measure, the US Armed Forces were required to prefer domestic suppliers so long as their prices were less than 50 per cent above the delivered price of foreign products, *excluding duty*; or less than 6 per cent above the foreign price inclusive of duty (OECD 1976, p. 127).

REFERENCES

ACARD (1986) *Medical Equipment*, London: HMSO.

Beesley, M. and Hamilton, R. (1984) 'Small firms seedbed role and the concept of turbulence', *Journal of Industrial Economics*, December, 217–32.

Carr, J. and Smith, L. (1985) 'How county hall promotes equality through its purchasing power', *Personnel Management*, May, 36–9.

Cmnd 4811 (1971) *Report of the Committee of Inquiry into Small Firms*, (Bolton), London: HMSO.

Cmnd 9227-I (1984) *Statement on the Defence Estimates 1984*, London: HMSO.

Cmnd 9867 (1986) *The General Electric Company PLC and the Plessey Company PLC*, Monopolies and Mergers Commission, London: HMSO.

Critchley, T. (1986) 'Buying the Critchley way', *Health Service Journal*, 13 November.

CSS (1986) *UK Military R&D*, Oxford: Oxford University Press.

Cunningham, M.T. and White, J.G. (1974) 'The behaviour of individual buyers in their search for suppliers of machine tools', *Journal of Management Studies*, May 115–28.

DHSS (1986) *Review of Artificial Limb and Appliance Centre Services*, the report of an independent working party under the chairmanship of Professor Ian McColl (two vols).

DTI (1985) *Tendering for Government Contracts*, advice for small firms, Department of Trade and Industry, London: HMSO.

EIU (1983) *The European Climate for Small Businesses*, a 10 country study, London: Economists Intelligence Unit.

Felch, R.I. (1985) 'Standards of conduct: the key to supplier relations', *Journal of Purchasing and Materials Management*, Fall, 16–18.

Forrester, J. and West, T. (1985) *Defence Sector Procurement: Opportunities for High Technology Small Firms*, Small Business Research Trust, London, September.

Government Purchasing (1984) Report to the Prime Minister, Cabinet Office, London: HMSO, December.

Harlow, C. (1983) *Commercial Interdependence: Public Corporations and Private Industry*, London: Policy Studies Institute, November.

Hartley, K. and Huby, M. (1985) 'Contracting-out in health and local authorities', *Public Money*, September, 23–6.

Hartley, K. and Hutton, J. (1982) *The Economics of the UK Medical Capital Equipment Market*, Research report to DHSS.

Hartley, K. and Tisdell, C. (1981) *Micro-Economic Policy*, London: J. Wiley.

HCP 399 (1986) Report from the Defence Committee, *Statement on the Defence Estimates 1986*, London: HMSO, June.

Kay, J., Meyer, C., and Thompson, D. (1986) *Privatisation and Regulation*, Oxford: Clarendon Press.

McGoldrick, P.J. and Douglas, R.A. (1983) 'Factors influencing the choice of a supplier by grocery distributors', *European Journal of Marketing* 5: 13–37.

Maddock, Sir I. (1983) *Civil Exploitation of Defence Technology*, London: NEDO.

Martin, S. (1983) 'Vertical relationships and industrial performance', *Quarterly Review of Economics and Business*, Spring, 6–18.

Maynard, A. and Hartley, K. (1984) 'The regulation of the pharmaceutical industry', in Lindren, B. (ed.), *Arne Ryde Symposium on Pharmaceutical Economics*, Swedish Institute for Health Economics.

MoD (1982) *The Transfer of Technology from Defence R&D to the Civil Sector*, Proceedings of a seminar, London: Procurement Executive, September.

MoD (1986) *Selling to the MoD*, London: Ministry of Defence.

NEDC (1982) *Policy for the UK Information Technology Industry*, London: NEDO.

NEDO (1975) *The Public Client and the Construction Industries*, London: HMSO.

OECD (1976) *Government Purchasing*, Regulations and procedures of OECD member countries, Paris: OECD.

PA (1986) *Defence Symposium*, summary of proceedings, London: PA Defence Services, November.

Parkinson, S.T. (1985) 'Factors influencing buyer-seller relationships in the market for high-technology products', *Journal of Business Research*, February, 49–60.

Rothwell, R. and Zegveld, W. (1981) *Industrial Innovation and Public Policy*, London: Frances Pinter.

Trinkous, J. and Corrin, M. (1984) 'Competitive advocacy to spare parts', *Journal of Purchasing and Materials Management*, Winter, 22–6.

Williamson, O.E. (1975) *Markets and Hierarchies: Analysis and Anti-Trust Implications*, New York: Free Press.

7

Small Firms' Merger Activity and Competition Policy

Alan Hughes

INTRODUCTION

The object of this chapter is to examine the impact of merger activity, restrictive trade practices, and competition policy upon the growth prospects of small firms[1] in the UK and upon their innovatory capacity. A central theme is that merger and inter-firm co-operation should be seen as part of a continuum of strategies available to large and small firms. Their impact upon small firms must therefore be evaluated in the light of the overall set of factors which condition small firms' growth prospects and which are the subject of other chapters. To keep this discussion within reasonable bounds it focuses as far as possible upon product market issues but inevitably touches upon the links between merger, restrictive trade practices, and competition policy on the one hand and, for example, capital market and management resource failures on the other.

These questions were considered in the report of the Bolton Committee on Small Firms which has served as a benchmark for much subsequent work on small firms in the UK (Bolton 1971; Moos 1971). The committee concluded that merger had contributed substantially to increases in industrial concentration which they associated with a reduction in the size of the small-firm sector and in its potential ability to contribute effectively as a breeding ground for new ideas and entrepreneurs. In their view mergers policy and restrictive trade practices policy had not been as helpful as they might have been in arresting this process, or in allowing small firms to combat dominant firm behaviour which unfairly damaged their competitive prospects. They argued that merger policy was neither tough enough nor rigorously enough enforced against large firms.

On the other hand they suggested that the application of restrictive trade practices policy, largely irrespective of the scale of the firms involved, had restricted the range of possibly desirable co-operative actions open to small firms in their attempts to compete effectively with oligopolistic market leaders. These themes have persisted and have received emphasis in recent debates in the UK over the impact of the current merger wave, and in the United States and the European Community in discussions over the role of joint ventures and inter-firm agreements in enhancing the contribution of small and medium-sized firms to innovation, productivity growth, and technical change. A framework for considering these questions is set out on pp. 130–3. We then consider the extent of small-firm involvement in merger activity in the UK, and trends in concentration and the size of the small-firm sector; the relative role of merger as a form of growth for small compared with larger firms; and the impact of merger upon the performance of small firms, including specifically the impact arising from the absorption of smaller firms within larger units. The role of co-operative agreements in small-firm development is discussed next along with possible inhibitions on desirable activities arising from UK policy in this area, and relevant developments in the restrictive trade practices legislation of the European Community. Finally some conclusions are presented. Appendix 7.1 sets out the principal relevant provisions of competition policy in the UK and the EEC relevant to the theme of this chapter and comments briefly on developments since the Bolton Report.

COMPETITION, MERGERS, RESTRICTIVE PRACTICES, AND SMALL FIRMS: SOME CONCEPTUAL ISSUES

The competitive process

In what follows, I will regard competition not as a state of affairs but as a dynamic process linking structural change with market behaviour. Competition is then a process of rivalry between producers, taking the form of contests within existing markets and potential entry into new areas. Competitive rivalry is conducted in terms of price, and product and process characteristics. It affects the rate of growth of technical change in products and processes, the rate of diffusion of new ideas across firms, as well as the allocation of resources between markets, and the evolution of market structures themselves. The opportunities for small-firm growth and development will therefore be conditioned by the technological opportunities available to them, their ability to exploit them, and the way in which structural and behavioural changes arising from competitive rivalry feed back onto these opportunities and abilities.[2]

In any given product market, at any given time, the size distribution of firms and the spread of efficiency across them will reflect past investment and growth, and will condition future growth and efficiency improvements. Firms with the lowest cost structures will have, *ceteris paribus*, the highest profits to finance competitive expansion, and will attempt to set a price which promises to attract customers and provide sufficient funds to pay for capacity expansion (either via retentions or attracting outside finance). Thus low-cost production will go with a competitive transfer of market share away from the least, towards the most efficient producers. Those threatened with an ever-diminishing market share must either innovate to get back into the competitive process by improving their efficiency, or gradually be driven out of business in their existing line of activity.

It is usual to think of this process as one in which firm sizes and market shares, and changes in them, are essentially dominated by the technical features of production and by production cost efficiency. The argument however may, in principle at least, be extended to encompass organizational and motivational issues internal to firms which condition their ability, or desire, to innovate successfully and hence their competitive strength (McEachern and Romeo 1978; Williamson 1975, 1970).

The transfer and innovation mechanisms are beneficial in the sense that they serve to improve the allocation of output between firms of differing efficiencies and spur the inefficient to improve their performance. Unless there are systematic tendencies leading to a loss of efficiency as firms expand or there is a very powerful innovation mechanism, then this competitive process will lead to increasing concentration and the gradual demise of unsuccessful and hence relatively small firms. In fact there are good reasons for thinking that recovering from past failures may be difficult, because although there may be a great incentive to adopt innovative recovery strategies, neither internal nor external

130

funding nor management ability may be available on a sufficient scale to allow it to take place.[3]

On the other hand, once the process of market concentration has proceeded sufficiently far to leave the bulk of production in the hands of a few dominant producers, then the transfer mechanism itself may lose some of its force as inter-dependence and gains from explicit or implicit collusion between the dominant producers become apparent. This may offer them both lower costs of competition and a higher market price to take advantage of any barriers to entry. The competitive process will then stagnate in conditions which will tend to inhibit new entry. There will be a reduction in the pressures leading to a reduced dispersion of efficiency and in the pressure to improve the level of efficiency itself. Thus large-firm behaviour and restrictive practices inhibit the entry and innovative growth of small firms.

Whilst there is sufficient evidence to suggest that the structure of industries evolves over their life-cycle along something like these lines, it is obviously a highly stylized description. It neglects for instance the role that buyers and suppliers can play in influencing structural trends. The pace of the process, and the survival of small firms in the face of it, varies considerably across markets. Forces on the supply side making it more likely that small firms will remain a significant element are: the absence of significant technical and other scale effects; insignificant learning effects; higher transport costs; low capital intensity of production; rapid technical change and the importance of flexible response to it; high exit and low entry barriers. On the demand side, small-firm survival is enhanced by specialist customer requirements; unstable demand coupled with high storage or inventory costs; and high personal service content. Small-firm birth and survival accordingly tends to be more significant in services as opposed to goods. These influences however also affect the cross-section distribution of small firms within manufacturing (Porter 1980; White 1982).

Dominant firm strategy, acquisition, and the scope for small-firm activity

Given the various structural features which predispose a market towards having a small-firm presence, the behaviour by the dominant group towards the small-firm fringes, and towards each other, will affect the evolution of both the structure and efficiency of the market and the growth opportunities for small firms. Where price leadership is practised and leads to higher industry prices then there may be scope for output share gains by the fringe of small firms or, if there are not major barriers to entry, by new producers as well. Thus there may be some pressure for dominant firm shares to erode (Worcester 1957; Utton 1986; Scherer 1980). However, the dominant firms' response to this may limit the opportunity for such recovery by new or small firms. They may for instance erect entry barriers (e.g. via product differentiation); introduce a limit-pricing strategy designed to restrict fringe and new firms to normal profits; maintain capacity to back up an implied threat of price war if small-firm expansion or new entry occurs; indulge in tactics designed to weaken small firms' competitive position, such as full line forcing and price discrimination; and, most relevant from our point of view, reassert dominance either by acquiring smaller rivals or by promoting restrictive trade agreements designed to stabilize market share – hence controlling the terms on which competitive rivalry may occur. If merger is to play this role a mechanism whereby the large can acquire the small, on terms that make it profitable to do so, must exist.

The degree of rivalry between dominant and smaller firms may also be affected by the strategies pursued by the latter. To the extent that small firms respond to the pressure of large-firm rivalry by seeking to segment the market and develop specific niches within it, then rivalry may occur more within the strategic market groups created than between them (Penrose 1959; Porter 1980). Competitive pressures on the large firms from small firms pursuing this strategy will therefore decline further. Small firms thus to some degree free themselves from the dominance of the large group and the further concentration of the market is impeded. The opportunities and prospects for small-firm growth, and the potential impact of merger and restrictive practices, can therefore vary widely depending upon the particular market circumstances in which they occur.

Small-firm strategy, acquisitions, and restrictive agreements

The discussion so far has tended to emphasize the bad effects on efficiency and small-firm prospects of merger and restrictive practices. It is clear, however, that co-operative or non-competitive activity may offer opportunities for small firms. Thus agreements to avoid duplicated innovative efforts, mount jointly financed research and development projects, or introduce standardization and specialization of products (giving cost efficiency through longer production runs) may revitalize their competitive prospects and hence the force of the innovation mechanism.

As with restrictive practices the impact of mergers in the competitive process is, in principle, ambiguous. Where a negative impact is assumed it is either based on the proposition that a horizontal merger between two firms in an industry will raise their joint market share (and thus by implication increase their desire and ability to indulge in anti-competitive behaviour towards smaller firms) or is based on the view that large firms end the growth prospects of small firms as independent units by acquiring them, with deleterious effects on their subsequent performance. This is not however the whole of the story. Just as with inter-firm agreements mergers between small and medium-sized firms may raise, rather than lower, the tempo of the competitive process if they produce efficiency gains through the avoidance of duplicated R&D efforts (Ordover and Willig 1985).

In more general terms merger offers an alternative to growth by internal investment for small as well as for large firms. Given external growth possibilities, merger, by reducing managerial services per unit of expansion, offers a way of pushing outwards the limits to growth arising from shortages of management resources (Penrose 1959). Merger may, of course, also enhance the external possibilities themselves if it offers scale or scope economies and enhances the competitive power of the firms involved. This may be especially significant if the scale curve is steepest in its early stages. It must be noted, however, that the effects, for instance, of scale itself cannot be a sufficient motive for merger since that is merely one way of achieving scale: internal growth is also possible. Thus auxiliary arguments in favour of a merger are required, stressing the speed and cost of the merger process compared with internal growth. Many of the issues here hinge on the nature of the competitive adjustment process and the gains for the small, as for the other firms, from learning by internal growth, as well as on management ability to control the acquisition process, and successfully effect the post merger changes necessary to ensure the efficiency gains (Williamson 1985; Kitching 1967, 1974; Samuels 1971; Hill 1984; Grinyer and Spender 1979; Cyert and George 1969).

There are a number of reasons however for expecting that the merger opportunities may differ between large and small firms. Thus, for instance, acquisition-intensive strategies may be easier for larger quoted as opposed to smaller unquoted companies since the targets of the latter will generally have to be willing to be absorbed. Takeover bids for unwilling targets with dispersed share ownership are a less-available option than for larger companies.

Analysis of small firms as recipients of takeover bids or merger offers from other firms, rather than as acquirers, usually emphasizes the problems of sustaining growth over the management life-cycle, the desire to capitalize on past efforts in order to meet retirement needs, and the inevitably associated impact of the tax system (Bolton 1971; Penrose 1959; Butters, Lintner, and Cary 1951). The opportunity to sell out is then an important element in the overall context in which entrepreneurs evaluate the advantages and disadvantages of funding and developing a business. It may be an important option open to owner-managers should the future growth and profitability of an established small firm become problematic because of external or internal constraints or because of changes in owner-management motivation. (Assuming that sale is not forced by 'unfair' competition from larger enterprises.) Where the pressure of the competitive process leads to decline through inefficient management then selling out to allow new management to take over may be a 'civilized alternative' to bankruptcy.

These emphases are in contrast to the bulk of the literature on large quoted company targets which has increasingly emphasized the disciplinary impact of takeover bids in the market for corporate control. Where small companies are not quoted and/or are closely held the likelihood of takeover against the wishes of owner-management is remote, and so is whatever impact on performance the disciplinary mechanism is believed to have.

Merger, concentration and small firms: market and hierarchy

Much of the literature on the impact of merger on the small-firm sector pays little attention to the positive aspects outlined above and has instead merely pointed to a link between merger activity and increased concentration at the market level. It is, of course, quite possible for the share of the largest 100 or 200 companies to be increasing whilst *within* the rest of the size distribution the small firms advance at a rate faster than those in the medium-size ranges; and, provided there is sufficient variance of growth rates across firms, for concentration to increase even though small firms *on average* grow faster than large firms or at the same rate (Hannah and Kay 1977; Prais 1976). It does not follow necessarily therefore that the largest firms must advance faster than, or at the expense of, the smaller firms with which this discussion is primarily concerned. Nor does it follow that such differences as do occur in large- and small-firm growth are caused primarily by a greater acquisition intensity of growth for larger than smaller firms. These are empirical questions and the answers to them may vary from time to time and industry to industry (Hannah and Kay 1977; Prais 1976; Hughes 1989).

Moreover, even where a pattern of large firms acquiring particular small ones does emerge, this may not be deleterious to the opportunities for small-firm growth generally. The sequential nature of the innovation process, for instance, from R&D through invention and innovation to the diffusion of new products and processes, imposes differing organizational and incentive requirements at different stages in the process and for different scales of firm (Burns and Stalker 1961; Rosenberg 1973; Freeman 1982; Williamson 1985). Thus within a given industry, or group of industries, there may be a complementariness between firms of different sizes specializing in different stages, and the optimal relationships between them may include a spectrum ranging from arm's length commercial transactions, through joint ventures, to minority shareholdings and ultimately majority ownership acquired by merger. The coexistence of firms of different sizes with differing interrelationships may therefore represent a mix of market and hierarchy suitable for particular technical conditions. Equally, once past an initial stage of development in an independent, small, flexible, informally structured organization, a new product or process may most effectively be taken further by the acquisition or integration of the smaller organization within a larger firm. There the continued involvement of the originators can be combined with access to the financial and marketing skills of the larger unit. Much will depend here, however, upon the ability of the larger organization to achieve its own input without adversely affecting creativity in the acquired enterprise. From the point of view of the larger firm the possibility of forming looser relationships with small firms, with a view to subsequently closer ownership ties, acts as stimulant to venture capital provision by the large firm. In that sense the possibility of merger could stimulate small, innovative, firm growth opportunities (Williamson 1970). Essentially, large firms come to play a role in filling a capital market gap, with merger and consequent ownership an inducement to them to behave in this way (Sargent 1981; Peach and Hargreaves 1976). Merger is then best seen as one element in a spectrum of institutional possibilities open to small firms with a desire to maintain their development, and to large firms seeking ways of maintaining their vitality and expanding their corporate portfolio.

In a given tax regime and set of relationships between finance and industry, with given rules governing co-operative arrangements between firms, and given the existing state of techniques in the internal management of organizations, merger may be the best way of dealing with some of the limits to continued growth and efficiency of small firms, and to their innovative behaviour in particular. Thus, for instance, the greater the legal restraints on joint venture or co-operative arrangements and the more efficient decentralizing flexible techniques for managing technical change are available, the greater the incentive to merger may be. Competition policy towards inter-firm agreements and mergers must therefore be flexible enough to accommodate beneficial effects flowing from them, and be interpreted in the context of their interrelationships with other institutional and economic forces bearing on small firms.

It would be helpful to have research undertaken specifically on the relative merits of the various possibilities discussed above. Unfortunately, the merger research literature has concentrated almost exclusively on large firms and their associated impacts and has tended to focus on simple financial performance comparisons between merging and non-merging firms as undifferentiated groups. However, the growing importance of conglomerate merger has led to some emphasis on internal aspects of corporate behaviour, and it is possible to draw a few inferences about small-merger impacts from the literature on mergers as a whole. This is attempted in the next section.

MERGER ACTIVITY AND SMALL FIRMS: EMPIRICAL EVIDENCE

Merger trends and characteristics in the UK

Table 7.1 sets out the principal characteristics of merger activity by UK commercial and industrial companies since 1969 in terms of acquisition expenditure and numbers of independent and subsidiary companies acquired at home and abroad. The value of expenditure is shown in money terms as well as deflated by stock market prices, and relative to gross domestic fixed capital formation. The table shows that after the merger boom of the late 1960s and early 1970s there was a long period of low activity in the period 1974–81 when the average annual expenditure on acquisition, the numbers of companies acquired and expenditure relative to capital formation were well below their previous levels. From 1984 onwards, however, expenditures at home and abroad rose substantially, culminating in the peak year of 1986. This increase was not matched by an increase in the numbers of acquisitions. Thus the current wave is characterized by relatively few, relatively massive mergers. In 1985, for instance, the largest 10 per cent of independent company acquisitions accounted for over 80 per cent of such total expenditures, whilst the largest 12 per cent of subsidiaries acquired accounted for over 70 per cent of such expenditures (see Table 7.2). The extreme skewness of the size distribution of target companies is also reflected in Table 7.3 which reports the results of an analysis of all proposed mergers involving financial and non-financial companies where either a regional or national market share of 25 per cent would have been created or increased, or where the gross assets of the target exceeded £30 million.

Running parallel with the increase in large-firm merger activity in recent years has been an increase in a decentralizing form of corporate activity; demerger by management buy-out, and the spin-off of subsidiaries (Coyne and Wright 1986) (see Tables 7.4, 7.5 and 7.6). This differs from the sale of subsidiaries between companies in Table 7.1 because it leads to the creation of new independent enterprises.

Table 7.1: Expenditure upon, and numbers of, acquisitions and mergers by industrial and commercial companies at home and abroad 1969–86

	Within the United Kingdom						Abroad³		Total	
					Sales of subsidiaries as a % of all acquisitions and mergers					
Year	Number	Expenditure £m	Expenditure¹ in 1962 Stock Market prices £m	Expenditure² as a % of gross fixed capital formation	number	expenditure	Number	Expenditure £m	Number	Expenditure £m
1969–73⁴	988	1388	777	38.6	21.6	13.0	66	95.4	1054	1483
1974–81	459	947	426	7.7	26.4	16.1	50	341.4	471	786
1982–86	529	6130	933	23.8	29.6	19.4	76	247.7	574	3044
1979	534	1656	620	10.4	21.9	11.2	63	344.8	597	2001
1980	469	1475	516	8.6	21.5	14.3	51	941.0	520	2416
1981	452	1144	355	6.6	27.7	22.9	150	762.2	602	1870
1982	463	2206	591	12.0	35.4	36.4	95	770.3	558	2976
1983	447	2343	497	12.9	31.8	18.6	71	387.1	505	2730
1984	568	5474	976	23.8	29.9	20.5	82	816.4	642	6290
1985	474	7090	1044	25.1	28.3	11.2	65	921.5	538	8022
1986	695	13535	1576	45.2	22.7	10.4	89	3333.1	784	16868

Sources

Economic Trends Supplement, National Income and Expenditure Annual Abstract, Financial Statistics, Business Monitor MQ7.

Notes

1 Actual Expenditure (usually the Stock Market value of the successful offer) deflated by the F.T. Actuaries 500 Industrial Share Index (1962 = 100).

2 Actual Expenditure as a percentage of GDFCF at current prices adjusted for leasing.

3 Overseas acquisition activity is likely to be understated because it excludes acquisitions and mergers overseas by existing overseas affiliates and subsidiaries of UK companies and because press coverage, on which the data is based, of overseas activity is less full than of domestic activity.

4 The first three rows are for annual averages for the periods shown.

Table 7.2: Size distribution of acquisitions and mergers of industrial and commercial companies within the UK in 1985 in terms of consideration paid

Expenditure £m		No	%	Expenditure	%
All acquisitions and mergers					
Total		474	100.0	7090	100.0
Over 25		38	8.0	5708	80.5
Over 10	up to 25	39	8.2	636	9.0
Over 5	up to 10	48	10.1	349	4.9
Over 2	up to 5	74	15.6	232	3.3
Over 1	up to 2	61	12.9	87	1.2
Over 0.5	up to 1	65	13.7	49	0.7
Over 0.1	up to 0.5	93	19.6	27	0.4
	0.1 or less	56	11.8	2	negl
Acquisitions and mergers of independent companies					
Total		340	100.0	6298	100.0
Over 25		31	9.1	5288	84.0
Over 10	up to 25	30	8.8	500	7.9
Over 5	up to 10	33	9.7	240	3.8
Over 2	up to 5	48	14.1	151	2.4
Over 1	up to 2	42	12.4	61	1.0
Over 0.5	up to 1	46	13.5	34	0.5
Over 0.1	up to 0.5	71	20.9	21	0.3
	0.1 or less	39	11.5	2	negl
Sales of subsidiaries between groups					
Total		134	100.0	793	100.0
Over 25		7	5.2	420	53.0
Over 10	up to 25	9	6.7	137	17.3
Over 5	up to 10	15	11.2	109	13.7
Over 2	up to 5	26	19.4	81	10.2
Over 1	up to 2	19	14.2	26	3.3
Over 0.5	up to 1	19	14.2	14	1.8
Over 0.1	up to 0.5	22	16.4	6	0.8
	0.1 or less	17	12.7	negl	negl

Source: Adapted from Business Monitor MQ7.Q3 1986 Table 6.

Table 7.3: Analysis by size of gross assets of proposed target companies in proposed mergers falling within the scope of the Mergers Panel in 1985

Size of assets £m	Number	% Total numbers	Assets £m	Average assets £m	% Total assets
0– 24.9	30	15.6	220	7.3	0.4
25– 49.9	49	25.5	1798	36.7	3.1
50– 99.9	31	16.1	2004	64.7	3.5
100–249.9	39	20.3	6085	156.0	10.6
250–499.9	22	11.5	7675	348.8	13.4
500–999.9	11	5.7	7617	692.5	13.2
1000 plus	10	5.2	32089	3208.9	55.8
Total	192	100.0	574888	299.4	100.0

Source: Annual Report of the Office of Fair Trading 1985. Adapted from Table 2, p. 58.

Table 7.4: Management buy-outs in the UK industrial and commercial sector, 1979–86

Year	No.	Total value £m	Average value £m
1977	13	–	–
1978	23	–	–
1979	52	26	0.50
1980	107	50	0.47
1981	124	114	0.92
1982	170	265	1.56
1983	205	315	1.54
1984	210	255	1.21
1985	279	1176	5.02
1986	140	710	5.07

Source: As for Table 7.5.

Table 7.5: Size distribution of management buy-outs in 1986

Size band £m	No.	%
less than 0.1	8	5.3
0.1 to 0.49	52	34.5
0.5 to 0.99	15	9.9
1.0 to 4.99	45	29.8
5.0 to 9.99	12	7.9
10.0 and over	19	12.6
Total	151	100.0

Source: Wright, M. and Coyne, J., *Management Buyouts in 1985*, Centre for Management Buy-out Research/Venture Economics, September 1986.

Table 7.6: Management buy-outs and UK manufacturing enterprises by employment size class 1979–80

Size of enterprise by no. of employees	Number of enterprises	%	Number of buy-outs	%
1–99	84229	93.9	51	46.4
100–199	2609	2.9	26	23.6
200–499	1543	1.7	25	22.7
500–999	609	0.7	8	7.3
1000 +	751	0.8	0	0
Total	89741	100.0	110	100.0

Source: Derived from Wright and Coyne (1986), Table 4.9.

Industrial concentration and the small-firm sector

In the two decades before the Bolton Report, market concentration in manufacturing in terms of employment grew rapidly. Thus between 1951 and 1958 it increased at about 0.4 per cent per annum, and between 1958 and 1968 at double that rate. Since then there has been stability in manufacturing but some tendency for increasing concentration in retailing (Hart and Clarke 1980; Clarke 1985; OFT 1985b).[4] A similar picture of rapid increases in the 1960s followed by stability since 1968 emerges for aggregate concentration in manufacturing and for the economy as a whole (Prais 1976; Hughes and Kumar 1984a, 1984b). As for

Table 7.7: Proportion of manufacturing employment in small[1] establishments in the UK and other countries 1963–79

Country	Time period		
	1963–6[2] %	1970–3[3] %	1977–9[4] %
UK	31	27	30 (24)[5]
W. Germany	34	31	31 (40)
US	39	38	39 (34)
Japan	54	62	68 (54)

Source: Adapted from Ganguly (1982) Tables 1 and 3.
Notes:
1 Small is defined as employing 1–199 employees.
2 Data for UK, W. Germany and US is for 1963, and for Japan is for 1966.
3 Data for UK and W. Germany is for 1973, for US is for 1972 and for Japan is for 1970.
4 Data for UK and W. Germany is for 1979, for US is for 1977 and for Japan is for 1978.
5 Data in brackets show share of establishments employing 20–199 employees.

Table 7.8: Employment by size cohort of firm, 1982–4, in the UK private sector

Size cohort	1982 Employment		1984 Employment		1982–4
	No. in millions	%	No. in millions	%	Change in % share
1–19	3.36	22.8	3.57	25.9	+ 3.2
20–49	1.57	10.6	1.57	11.4	+ 0.8
50–99	1.20	8.1	1.15	8.3	+ 0.2
100–499	2.84	19.2	2.45	17.8	− 1.4
500–999	1.25	8.5	1.06	7.7	− 0.7
1000 +	4.55	30.8	4.00	29.0	− 1.8
All	14.77	100.0	13.80	100.0	0.0

Source: Calculated from Gallagher and Doyle (1986) Figure 2.

trends in the share of the small-firm sector itself, it appears that, at least in terms of employment in manufacturing, the long-term decline to the mid 1960s identified by Bolton was arrested in the UK in the 1970s when the growth in concentration slowed down. Thus Table 7.7 shows that in the UK the share of small establishments employing between 1 and 200 people fell from 31 per cent to 27 per cent in the decade 1963–73 but rose back to 30 per cent by the end of the 1970s whilst there was stability in West Germany and the US. Interpreting developments since then is made difficult by the impact of recession and the paucity of reliable data. In manufacturing the Census of Production data in Figure 7.1 show that employment in firms employing less than 100 and those employing between 100 and 500 has drifted upwards since the late 1970s. Figure 7.2 shows however that this reflects a substantial fall in employment in larger firms rather than a growth in employment in smaller ones (Storey and Johnson 1987a). Gallagher and Doyle (1986) for the period 1982–4 suggest a similar upward drift especially in the share of firms employing 1 to 20 people in the private sector taken as a whole, in this case combined with an absolute increase in their employment. These results, shown in Table 7.8, are however very sensitive to adjustments which are necessary to deal with biases in their underlying raw data for the smallest categories of firms (see for instance the discussion in Storey and Johnson (1987b), and Hart (1987) suggesting an upward bias in Gallagher and Doyle's results).

The suggestion that there has been a recent resurgence in small firm activity in manufacturing is reinforced by Census of Production data on net output shares. Firms employing fewer than 100 workers in 1954 accounts for around 22 per cent of total manufacturing employment. This share fell to 18 per cent in 1963. By the mid-1980s it had recovered to around 23 per cent. Similarly to the business sector as a whole, Table 7.9 shows that between 1978/9 and 1985, there was a decline in numbers of large units with a turnover of £2 million or more and an increase in the turnover categories of £100,000 or less. There are, however, problems of interpretation here, because of the inclusion of subsidiary as well as parent companies.

Figure 7.1: Employment distribution in manufacturing by firm size, 1971–82

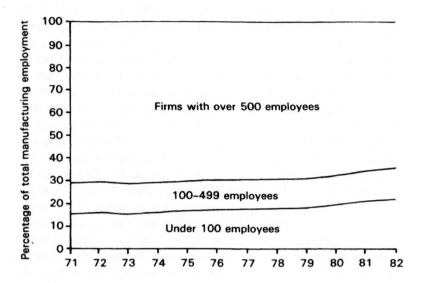

Source: Storey and Johnson (1987a).

Figure 7.2: Manufacturing employment by firm size, 1971–82

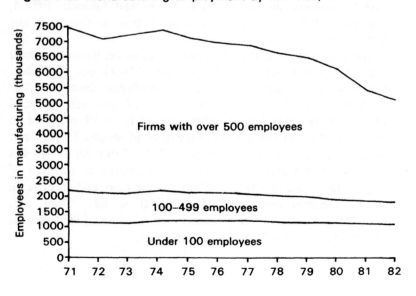

Source: Storey and Johnson (1987a).

Table 7.9: The percentage distribution of business units by turnover size band, 1978–9 and 1985

Turnover[1] size band (£000) in 1985 prices	% Number of business units		Change in % share
	1978/9	1985	
0–19	10	16	+ 6
29–99	50	53	+ 3
200–999	34	27	− 7
1,000–1,999	3	2	− 1
2,000 +	3	3	0
Total	100	100	
Total number of business units	1,331,681	15,323,156	

Source: Adapted from *British Business* 23 January 1981 Table 1, Business Monitor PA 1003 1986 Table 2.

Small firms as acquirers

The evidence on small-firm acquisition behaviour is scattered and unsystematic. Around 5 per cent of the Bolton Report's manufacturing sample of 1,600 firms employing less than 200 people made acquisitions in the period 1964–9, and around 4 per cent of their 1,800 non-manufacturing population did. Within these samples merger was more prevalent amongst those employing more than 100, and was associated with relatively fast growth companies (Table 7.10). This simply indicates the event of one or more acquisitions and cannot tell us much about the *relative* importance of merger compared with internal growth by size of firm. That would require data on the size of the acquisitions and their frequency by company. Neither is it possible to compare this directly with the experience of larger companies.[5]

Within the quoted sector in the UK there is some evidence to suggest that the smaller firms are more merger-intensive in their growth than larger ones (Utton 1972; Meeks 1977). This may reflect the scale of acquisition necessary by big firms to maintain a given proportionate growth by merger; inhibitions arising from competition policy; the costs of acquisition battles against reluctant giant targets; and management integration problems. This

145

Table 7.10: Percentage of independent small companies in 1969 making acquisition in the previous five years, by size and rate of growth of acquiring company

No. of employees	Manufacturing		Non-manufacturing	
	Total of firms in sample	% Acquiring	Total of firms in sample	% Acquiring
1–24	–	3	–	n.a.
25–29	–	9	–	n.a.
100–199	–	18	–	n.a.
All	1607	5	1808	4
Rate of growth				
Fast (>90% growth in turnover)	190	16	193	11
Slow (<90% growth in turnover)	315	5	281	3

Source: Bolton (1971, 1972).

pattern seems to vary during merger waves however when 'whale eats whale' mergers tend to increase in importance (Hughes 1989). Mergers are thus clearly a part of small-firm growth strategies, but we do not have a study of them which analyses their role in any detail.

Small firms as targets

Although, as we have seen (Table 7.2), the vast majority of acquired companies are to be found in the smallest size classes, merger is neither as important a form of 'death' nor as prevalent per head of the population for small firms as for large ones. Thus whereas in the 1960s and 1970s acquisitions accounted for between 80 per cent and 90 per cent of large quoted company deaths (Singh 1975; Kuehn 1975; Samuels and Chesher 1972) it accounted for only 60 per cent of deaths in the Bolton small-firm population (Table 7.11). Moreover, within the quoted population the smallest size classes have, along with the very largest companies, the lowest probability of being acquired (Singh 1975; Kuehn 1975; Davies and Kuehn 1977). Data on differences in

Table 7.11: Mortality ratios: percentage of 1963 population of independent small companies dying by 1970 by cause of death

Type of death	Manufacturing and construction %	Wholesaling %	Motor trade %	Retailing %
Voluntary liquidation	5	15	5	7
Compulsory liquidation	3	4	3	8
Ceased trading	2	6	5	9
Taken over	13	8	5	4
All deaths	23	33	19	28
Taken over as % of all deaths	57	24	26	14

Source: Merret Cyriax Associates (1971).

merger death *rates* between the quoted and non-quoted or small-firm sector are not directly available. Around a quarter of the Bolton small-firm sample was acquired between 1963 and 1970 suggesting an annual average merger death rate of around 3 per cent (similiar to the 2 per cent to 3 per cent reported for a different sample of small firms in the 1960s by Boswell 1972). This is of the same magnitude as rates for the smallest 20 per cent of a quoted company sample for the period 1967–70, and less than the rates for all except the top 10 per cent and 5 per cent by size (Singh 1975).

The evidence on attitudes to selling out and the motivations behind actual sales are broadly consistent with the emphases noted on pp. 131–6. Thus over 50 per cent of a sample of East Midlands private companies employing less than 500 people in the engineering hosiery and knitwear industries in the late 1960s reported that they had an open-minded or positive attitude towards the prospect of being taken over (Boswell 1972). Amongst this 40 per cent, the desire for capital gains for retirement was the most frequently cited reason, and this was so whether the company was young, middle-, or old-aged. (Old-aged = 70 years since formation, middle-aged = 20–40 years, young = less than 20 years). Next most important was the need for management succession which, as might be expected, was most prevalent amongst the middle-aged group of companies (the younger ones not having to face the problem yet, and the older ones having perhaps already made an adjustment.) Pressure from a weak competitive position was a factor only for the old-aged firms. These data are of course for a small sample of firms and may be spatially, historically, and industrially specific. They also relate to attitudes towards takeover rather than the characteristics of the actual event. These may differ not least because the desires of buyers as well as sellers come into play. The scattered evidence suggests that younger firms appear more vulnerable than older firms (Boswell 1972), and although management succession problems are cited as a major factor in actual as well as prospective takeovers, they run second to financial difficulties (Table 7.12). The companies acquiring the younger smaller concerns seem to be small or medium-sized quoted companies (e.g. employing less than 2,000 people). There is not much evidence of substantial management change following takeover (Boswell 1972). All of this is however based on relatively impressionistic data. Just as with acquisition behaviour we have no systematic study of the motivation behind takeovers with small firms as targets. In particular we have no study which attempts to relate merger behaviour to other features of the small-firm environment which restrict or otherwise affect their prospects.

Effects of merger on small-firm performance

The central conceptual problem in assessing the impact of merger on company performance lies in judging what would have happened in its absence. There are a number of studies which compare the performance of merging firms relative to industry averages before merger with their relative performance afterwards, in terms of profitability and investment; a small number measuring real resource effects, and a growing literature on the impact of merger on company share prices (Meeks 1977; Cowling *et al.* 1980; Mueller 1980; Hughes 1989). In general this literature suggests neutral or small negative performance impacts *on average*, taking all mergers as a single group. The size of the target on its own seems to make little difference, nor the size of the acquirer. None of these studies is however designed to provide direct evidence on the performance of small firms after merger either as targets or acquirers. A few inferences may none

Table 7.12: Independent companies taken over, 1963–70, by cause of takeover

Reason for takeover	Manufacturing and construction %	Whole-saling %	Motor trade %	Retailing %
Financial failure	37	45	33	6
Management succession problems	24	32	13	33
Vertical integration: tying in suppliers	11	–	–	–
Vertical integration: tying in outlets	–	–	45	61
To eliminate competition	14	–	9	–
Estate duty payments	14	–	–	–
Other tax reasons	–	23	–	–
All	100			

Source: Merret Cyriax Associates (1971).

the less be drawn. One tentative conclusion which is suggested by the evidence from the UK is that non-horizontal mergers have less negative or more positive impacts on profits and investment than horizontal mergers. Non-horizontal mergers are also somewhat more likely to involve the acquisition of superior-performing, small companies, rather than average or below-par performing larger ones (Hughes 1989; Kumar 1984; Meeks 1977; Cosh, Hughes, and Singh 1980). Finally, post-merger success in merger generally, and non-horizontal merger in particular, may be critically affected by the way their management integration and planning is carried out (Kitching 1967, 1974; Grinyer and Spender 1979; Samuels 1971; Hill and Pickering 1986). Diversifying divisionalized concerns and acquiring smaller dynamic companies may with effective management sustain and improve performance. This is however only one possible outcome and there is simply no systematic research specifically designed to sort out the possible interrelationships or to distinguish between those mergers which succeed and those which fail, either for mergers in general or small-firm mergers in particular. Nor does any of this literature concern itself with innovation or go far in disentangling the actual performance of small firms after merger once they have been absorbed into the consolidated accounts of larger organizations. That things do not always work out as planned, and that the bits of the jigsaw do not always fit together, is reflected in the divestment and sales of subsidiaries noted earlier, and in the development of corporate buy-outs, although this is clearly also sensitive to the legislative and tax regime in operation and macroeconomic demand conditions. There is also some evidence from the United States suggesting that life after takeover can be unproductive – especially where key technical management personnel find it uncongenial to have a flexible, or otherwise favourable, innovative corporate culture replaced by a more restrictive short-term, or cash-flow, oriented one (Scherer and Ravenscraft 1984; Rhoades 1983; Williamson 1985; Mueller 1986). An example of this is provided by the acquisition of Houston Oil by Tenneco in 1980. Tenneco at that time was a large US conglomerate with sales of over \$15 billion and employees numbering over 100,000; Houston was a technically sophisticated oil exploration company employing around 1,200 people and with sales pre-merger of \$383 million. Within a year between a fifth and one-third of various categories of top management and scientific manpower left Houston because of bureaucratic difficulties over incentive systems and payment structures (cited in Williamson 1985). The importance of an appropriately organic and flexible framework for dealing with innovative and fast-changing markets is well known (Burns and Stalker 1961). Difficulties of achieving this within larger organizations therefore have led to the development of different systems of combining the activity of large and small ventures in innovation and R&D intensive areas. This has happened either through the development of intrapreneurship, or via joint venture and minority shareholder arrangements with small enterprises, in preference to merger and in-house management. For example, General Motors purchased 11 per cent of a small company, Teknowledge, in 1984 on the grounds that 'if we purchased such a company outright we would kill the goose that laid the golden egg' (cited in Williamson 1985). As an example of intrapreneurship, Rank Xerox has offered around 250 individual employees the opportunity to set up business as an independent limited company contracting (up to 50 per cent of their output) on commercial terms for parent company business (Hornby 1986).

Merger as a way of achieving technology transfer is in general relatively unexplored. Lowe and Crawford (1984) found only 4 out of a sample of 20 companies using the merger route to acquire technology in the early 1980s. Other routes involved buying in personnel, joint collaborative R&D, in-house imitation, plant purchase, sub-contracting and most frequently technology licensing.

In sum, while there is a great deal of speculation about the impact of merger on small-firm performance, there is very little hard evidence on which to base any conclusion or policy recommendation.

CO-OPERATION AND RESTRICTIVE AGREEMENTS: SOME EXAMPLES

A number of arguments were set out earlier for expecting that the efficiency-enhancing role of small firms in the competitive process may benefit from certain kinds of agreements between them. Some of these agreements might have significant restrictions on rivalry between the parties to them and others not. There is no research literature bearing directly on the question of what sorts of inter-firm agreements are especially suitable for the promotion of innovative and sustained growth by small firms, nor on what particular aspects of UK competition legislation environment most inhibit suitable arrangements. It is possible however to give some examples from EEC and other countries of cases which illustrate the kinds of benefits claimed.

Specialization agreements reduce the numbers of producers in a market but allow those remaining to gain from long production runs. Thus in the 1969 Clima-Chappé-Buderus Agreement (exempted by the European Commission from the prohibition on anti-competitive agreements of the EEC), a French and a German producer rationalized their production of air-conditioning equipment, supplied each other with the lines each had dropped and became exclusive distributors on their home markets (Swann 1983). Crisis cartels may also lead to efficient rationalization of capacity to the benefit of smaller firms. Thus in 1983, under the competition law of the Federal Republic of Germany, 28 domestic steel reinforcement fabric makers with a combined market share of 90 per cent were permitted to agree on a three-year phased reduction of capacity. In reporting this the authorities noted that

151

the industry consisted of a group of small and medium-sized companies and a small number of giant enterprises. They commented that 'the competitiveness of the first group against its larger competitors can in the long run only be ensured by a systematic capacity reduction by all enterprises involved' (OECD 1986).

The gains from collaborative research and development have been touched upon earlier and are recognized in the block exemption procedure for such schemes embodied in the competition policy legislation of the EEC. In addition to decisions on individual cases, the Commission has emphasized that certain kinds of agreements can be beneficial even where competition is restricted, and has put into effect regulations exempting them as classes of agreement from the anti-competitive prohibitions of Article 86(1) of the Treaty of Rome. This is regarded as especially beneficial for small and medium-sized enterprises because of the speed of the procedures in qualifying for exemption, and because the kinds of agreement exempted are especially relevant for them. They include, for instance, patent licensing agreements with small firms as licensees; specialization agreements where joint market shares are less than 20 per cent and turnover is less than 500 million ECU; and joint research and development and joint exploitation agreements with the same 20 per cent coverage or less (see the Appendix, p. 153, for further details).

Although the possibility of benefits arising from small-firm co-operation are clearly recognized in policy arrangements such as these, there is very little systematic, theoretical or empirical literature bearing on them. What little there is suggests beneficial effects from suppressing duplicated R&D efforts. Problems of controlling and administering collaborative agreements and keeping the individual company incentive structure keen enough to put effort and resources into the joint endeavour may lead to merger being a preferable option (Ordover and Willig 1985).

An examination of the extent and effect of agreements involving small firms in the EEC and of the extent to which, if at all, desirable innovative strategies are inhibited by the Restrictive Trade Practices legislation of the UK seems worth pursuing.

CONCLUSIONS

Despite the continued concern that mergers by large firms may inhibit the growth and innovatory prospects of small firms, there is very little direct evidence which bears on the issue raised. In principle it is clear that in certain circumstances mergers between large and small firms, and between small firms themselves, may beneficially affect the performance of the formerly separate units. We have no recent evidence, or any systematic study of small firms, which can tell us what the actual effects are, on average. Whilst the general literature on merger impacts suggests that merger policy should be carefully enforced, nothing specific emerges from our discussion of small-firm involvement in merger to suggest specific policy recommendations. It is clear enough, however, that since in principle there are circumstances where mergers involving large and small firms may be beneficial, policy proposals involving unqualified bans on mergers by larger firms would be unduly restrictive. At an aggregate level it is noticeable that the period of intense merger activity in the period 1968–73 was not associated, in the short term at least, with either an increase in concentration or a decline in the small-firm sector.

As with mergers, circumstances can be identified in which inter-firm agreements which restrict competitive rivalry may also be beneficial for small-firm growth prospects. Restrictive Trade Practices policy must be flexible enough to permit this. As with mergers, however, we have little in the way of systematic evidence to guide us more specifically.

There is scope for new empirical work on the extent of both merger and co-operative inter-firm behaviour involving small firms and their impact on small-firm growth and innovatory capacity.

APPENDIX 7.1
COMPETITION POLICY IN THE UK AND THE EEC AND THE RECOMMENDATIONS OF THE BOLTON REPORT

Current legislation in the UK

At present, small firms may be influenced by UK competition policy in four main ways.[6] These arise from: legislation against restrictive agreements and resale price maintenance contained in the Restrictive Trade Practices Acts of 1976 and 1977 and in the Resale Prices Act of 1976; legislation governing monopoly and merger contained in the Fair Trading Act 1973; and legislation seeking to control individual anti-competitive practices by companies not necessarily occupying monopoly or dominant market position contained in the Competition Act 1980. Competition policy is currently under review (HMSO 1988a, 1998b).

Restrictive practices and resale price maintenance

Under the restrictive trade practices legislation the following broad categories of agreement between two or more parties are statutorily subject to registration on a register maintained by the Director General of Fair Trading (DGFT):[7]

(i) Agreements where one or more parties in business in the UK, (when acquiring as well as supplying) accept limitations on their freedom of action concerning prices (including, since 1973, prices to be recommended), conditions of sale, customers, quantities or descriptions, processes of manufacture.

(ii) (Since 1969) agreements providing for furnishing of information about prices or terms and conditions of supply, except to 'specified authorities' (e.g. Government or NEDO).

It is important to note that registrability depends on the *form* of restriction contained in an agreement and not on whether the effect of the agreement is anti-competitive.[8]

Each restrictive agreement is subject to judicial examination in the Restrictive Practices Court[9] (a division of the High Court) unless under Section 21(2) of the Act the DGFT represents to the Secretary of State that its effect on competition is insignificant and the Secretary of State gives a direction to the DGFT relieving him of his duty to refer the agreement to the Court. It does, however, remain on the public register.[10]

For an agreement going before the Court there is an initial presumption that its provisions are against the public interest, and it is up to the parties to the agreement to persuade the Court that the agreement nevertheless works in the public interest, in one or more of the following respects (the so-called 'gateways', presented here in summary form):

(i) Protecting the public from injury.

(ii) Benefiting the public, as purchasers, consumers, or users.

(iii) Acting as a necessary countervailing influence against anti-competitive activities of a third party.

(iv) Needed to secure fair terms from a monopolist.

(v) Preventing local unemployment.

(vi) Significantly promoting exports.

(vii) Needed to support other restrictions or information provisions previously found acceptable to the Court.

(viii) (Since 1968) not materially restricting or discouraging competition.

An agreement failing to pass through any of these gateways is automatically struck down. However, even if one or more gateways are passed through, the Court has still to determine whether, on balance, the agreement works for or against the public interest. If for, the agreement may remain in operation (or, if it was temporarily prohibited pending the Court's decision, it may be put into operation). If any restrictions or information provisions are found to be against the public interest, they are struck down and may not be replaced by others 'to the like effect'.

All agreements remain on the register, whether or not they have been struck down, or terminated for any other reason. By 1985, there were 4,342 agreements relating to goods on the register, and 1,153 relating to services.

A review of restrictive trade practices policy in the UK (HMSO 1979) concluded that the legislation was too inflexible and argued that it was possible that desirable agreements which had significant or insignificant competitive effects might be deterred by it. It was also argued that it failed to deal with significant anti-competitive behaviour which did not take the form of a registrable agreement, especially single-firm practices by concerns not falling within the statutory criteria necessary to permit investigation under monopoly legislation. This argument produced a recommendation for specific legislation to deal with such anti-competitive practices. This was subsequently embodied in the 1980 Competition Act (see further below). More directly relevant to the possible adverse impact of the legislation on small firms and in relation to the argument about inflexibility and desirable agreements the report suggested *inter alia*:

(i) A two-part registration procedure giving the DGFT greater discretion not to proceed in insignificant cases.

155

(ii) Power to be given to the DGFT to approve cases without taking them to the Court for adjudication.

(iii) Exemption from the legislation for trade association recommended codes of practice which were sponsored by the OFT.

(iv) Amendments to the Act to permit trade-associated recommendations to be individually treated as separate agreements (so as to avoid referring a whole agreement instead of the offending part).

None of these recommendations was embodied in the 1980 Competition Act legislation. The annual report of the DGFT for 1980 (HMSO) did however set out the features of some agreements which had led to directions being sought for section 21(2) exemptions, some of which are clearly relevant to small firms:

> Certain types of agreement – those containing restrictions involving price fixing or collusive tendering arrangements – are regarded at a very early stage as unsuitable for section 21(2) and, indeed, in many cases such agreements are referred to the Court even if all the restrictions are abandoned by the parties after registration. Other types of restriction, depending on the circumstances, have a significant effect on competition and it is with a view to identifying these and seeking either their abandonment or their defence before the Court that the detailed investigations carried out by the Office are often directed. Even where restrictions appear at first sight to have no significant effect on competition, it is often necessary to consult various interests to see whether the restrictions are likely to be detrimental in any way.
>
> A number of agreements considered for a section 21(2) representation are, of course, *sui generis*, but in recent years, including 1980, the following features have occurred in some of the common types of agreement subject to investigation and have often met the criteria for directions.

Joint ventures

A number of agreements for new joint ventures have been submitted to the Office. Directions have been given on certain of these where the restrictions are the minimum necessary for the joint venture and do not unduly restrict the parties or the joint venture. Joint ventures commonly include restrictions on the parent companies not to compete with the joint venture. In assessing the significance of such restrictions, the Office looks to see that there is clear evidence of competition in the relevant market from other suppliers or from other substitute goods or services, and that no evidence of possible detriments to third parties has been forthcoming. A number of joint ventures which did not initially meet these criteria have been modified.

Codes of practice

Several of the agreements concerning trade associations and some professional bodies not exempted from the legislation contain codes of practice or conduct for their members. In some cases the codes have been introduced in consultation with the Office, and the implications of the Act to their provisions considered in advance, so that this aspect of an agreement is immediately suitable for a representation.

Where, however, codes of practice are already in operation, they frequently contain provisions for self-regulation which have the effect of imposing significant restrictions on competition, and these must be modified or abandoned in an agreement if it is to be considered for a representation. Examples of such restrictions are those on advertising, canvassing for business, and on remuneration.

Standard terms and conditions

The recommendations by trade associations of standard terms and conditions for the supply or acquisition of goods or services is a common practice. Standard terms and conditions may often be desirable in the interests of both supplier and customer, especially where comparatively small firms with little or no legal expertise are concerned, as otherwise many contracts might be entered into which are not enforceable at law. The 1979 report stated that the recommendation of standard terms and conditions by an association is not regarded as necessarily having a significant effect on competition but, to ensure there is no likely detriment, the terms should be fair and reasonable to all concerned, not likely to mislead those who will use them, and not unnecessarily exclude variation to meet special circumstances and requirements. The benefit to customers of having standard conditions must be balanced against any detriment to them of being deprived of the freedom to secure more favourable terms than those likely to result from the restrictions imposed by them. In general, mandatory standard terms and

157

conditions are not regarded as suitable for section 21(2) since they are not variable to meet special circumstances. In all cases the recommended terms and conditions are looked at clause by clause.

Agreements with contractual clauses void under the Unfair Contract Terms Act are not acceptable for a section 21(2) representation.

Provisions as to contractual liability for loss or damage were referred to in last year's report. In considering whether the limitation of liability recommended by an association to its members is acceptable depends very much on individual circumstances. For instance, it may be more economical for the customer to provide insurance cover, for the supplier to accept less liability, and for this to be reflected in the charge. In some cases, notably in respect of carriage and storage services, some customers are already covered by their own insurance at all stages. It might be reasonable for the association to recommend standard terms and conditions which offer several options as to acceptance of liability, depending on the insurance required by the customer and the charge to be made for the service.

A further question that sometimes arises in liability clauses, in particular in the services field, is whether it would be appropriate to include a recommended level of compensation for small claims, or for the contractor to accept liability up to a declared value, to be proved in the event of a claim. Proposals of this sort are still under discussion with the Office.

Another feature of some standard terms and conditions is provision for surcharges on overdue accounts. Where specific rates of interest are provided, it is often difficult to assess what is reasonable. What is appropriate depends on the varying circumstances of the trade or industry and would need to be justified by the association as a genuine pre-estimate of loss. The Office would not be able to make a representation on any surcharge which included an element of penalty.

Group buying organizations

There is a number of group buying organizations, mainly but not entirely in the grocery field, where the provisions agreed by the members of their operation involve registrable restrictions. Most, but not all, of the agreements relating to these 'voluntary groups' are not subject to directions; one or two are, however, still under consideration. Restrictions which are common to many groups are those whereby the group recommends prices for goods covered by special promotions and/or for its 'own brand' goods. As long as members are free to charge lower prices if they wish and, in the case of promotions, provided that the recommended prices are lower than those normally charged outside promotions and the promotions are of short duration, these restrictions (although they involve prices) have not been regarded as significant.

Other restrictions have appeared in agreements of these groups and some have had to be abandoned or modified before representations could be made.

Those not found acceptable included allocation of geographical areas to particular members, wholesalers not to supply or sponsor retailers outside defined areas, wholesalers not to sponsor two or more retailers who would be in direct competition with each other, wholesalers or retailers to purchase minimum quantities through the group, and members not to join any other group.

Some agreements relating to 'cash and carry' wholesalers have included a ban on their supplying the general public. These have had to be modified to allow individual wholesalers freedom to decide for themselves whom they will supply – though in many cases there are local authority regulations which prevent wholesale warehouses from supplying anyone other than bona fide trade customers.   (OFT 1980)

Since 1980, a further review of Restrictive Trade Practices policy has been undertaken and a consultative document (HMSO 1988a) published proposing a major overhaul of the existing system. This is intended to shift the UK towards EEC practice. Irrespective of their form, anti-competitive agreements would be prohibited. Exemptions would be possible but via an administrative rather that a judicial process. (See further below on the EEC system).

Monopolies

Under the terms of the Fair Trading Act of 1973 a firm may be referred by the Director General of Fair Trading (subject to a public veto by the Secretary of State) for investigation by the Monopolies and Mergers Commission of its activities where at least 25 per cent of all goods or services of a particular description supplied in that UK market (or a substantial part of it) are supplied by, or to, the company concerned; or where the company is one of two or more firms who are conducting their affairs so as to restrict or distort competition with regard to such a proportion of the market (i.e. a complex monopoly).

References to the Monopolies and Mergers Commission are made by the DGFT (subject to public veto by the Secretary of State) and by Ministers. Nationalized industries may only be referred by the Secretary of State and the Minister concerned.

A reference takes the form of requiring the Commission to investigate and report (since 1973 usually within a limited time – typically 10 to 24 months) on whether, and in what form, a monopoly situation exists and, usually also, whether, and in what way, it is being maintained or exploited contrary to the public interest. A limited reference may be made where, once the monopoly has been established, the Commission is restricted to considering the consequences of one or more specified monopolistic practices.

In carrying out its investigations, the Commission is asked to take into account the desirability of:

(i) Effective competition.[11]

(ii) Promoting consumers', purchasers', and other users' interests with regard to price, quality, and variety.

(iii) Promoting (via competition) cost-reduction, new techniques and products, and entry of new competitors into the market.

(iv) A balanced distribution of industry and employment.

(v) Competition abroad, among UK suppliers.

The Commission reports to the government department responsible. If the report is accepted and it has come out against particular monopolistic practices, these may be acted against by statutory order[12] or (more usually) by obtaining undertakings from the firm(s) concerned. The DGFT advises the Minister on follow-up action and usually carries it forward, at the request of the Minister.[13] The Monopolies Commission at present takes a broadly neutral stance on large-firm dominance. Unlike the position taken with respect to restrictive practices, there is no prior presumption that concentrated *structures* are against the public interest.

Anti-competitive practices

Since 1980 a firm may be investigated by the Director General of Fair Trading to establish whether it is engaged in anti-competitive practices involving neither registrable agreements with other firms nor a dominant statutory monopoly position in the market or markets concerned. For this purpose the 1980 Act defines as an anti-competitive practice by an individual firm a course of conduct which has, or is likely to have, or is intended to have, the effect of restricting, preventing, or distorting competition in connection with the production, supply, or acquisition of goods in the UK or any part of it. If the Director General finds that an anti-competitive practice is being followed, then he may either accept undertakings by the firm to stop or modify the practice, or refer it to the Monopolies and Mergers Commission for a further investigation to establish whether or not the practice is against the public interest.[14] If found against the public interest by the Monopolies and Mergers Commission, then orders may be made or undertakings obtained to stop or modify the practice concerned.

Mergers

Mergers between firms are subject to the provisions of the Fair Trading Act of 1973, whereby a merger may be referred to the Monopolies and Mergers Commission if it creates or intensifies a monopoly situation as defined above, or where (since 1984) at least £30m worth of assets are being taken over. Just as for monopolies, the Commission (since 1973) may be asked to concentrate on particular aspects of the merger.

The powers for making a reference to the Commission are reserved to the Secretary of State, though he is advised by the DGFT who is Chairman of the inter-departmental Mergers Panel, which scrutinizes mergers falling within the provisions of the Act and can recommend to the Secretary of State that those merger proposals which raise substantial issues of public interest be referred to the Commission.

There is no pre-notification scheme, and mergers can be referred up to six months after they have taken place. The maximum period for report is six months (with a possibility of a further three months' extension in special circumstances) and a 'standstill' order may be made for this period if the merger is not already complete. In practice, such orders are not usually necessary.

The Commission, in determining whether or not to recommend that the merger should be allowed to proceed (or be dissolved), takes into account the same public interest criteria as for monopolies. As with monopolies, there is no presumption that they are against the public interest.

As a result of recent review of merger policy, it has been proposed (HMSO 1988b) that a formal but non-mandatory pre-notification scheme should be introduced, and that procedures should be adopted both to speed up referral and investigation and to increase the powers of the DGFT to obtain undertakings (including post-merger divestments) designed to remove threats to competition arising in proposed mergers.

Competition policy and the recommendations of the Bolton Report

The authors of the Bolton Report concluded that 'there is some reason to believe that small firms have benefited less than might have been hoped from the Monopolies and Mergers legislation, and, that from the Restrictive Trade Practices Acts, they have suffered certain needless disabilities' (Bolton 1971, §16.3, p. 283. See also Moos (1971) *passim*). They argued that the decline in the small-firm sector was linked to the growth in industrial concentration and associated dominant firm behaviour. This stimulated concentration in supplier and customer industries through bulk purchasing activities and generally raised entry barriers to small firms (Bolton 1971, §7.2.24). They thought these developments would weaken the positive role that a healthy small-firm sector could play in providing actual or potential competition to large multiproduct dominant firms; stimulating innovation; and providing a breeding ground for new entrepreneurial talent.

They therefore concluded there should be an emphasis in monopoly and merger policy on the importance of maintaining a balanced industrial structure, by which they meant that 'there should in each industry be a substantial force of small firms (constantly reinforced by new starters) some of which may be expected to grow into serious rivals to the present major competitors' (Bolton 1971, p. 49). Thus monopoly and merger policy should be more vigorously enforced and the virtue of maintaining a balanced structure in this sense emphasized in setting out the matters that should be borne in mind in assessing the merits of mergers. They also argued that close attention should be paid to behaviour (such as refusal to supply and price discrimination) designed to restrict the competitive challenge of small firms, and they recommended a referral of this question to the Monopolies Commission for a general report.

As far as rivalry between small firms themselves was concerned however the Bolton Report argued that it was not 'anything like so clear that intense competition needs to be preserved as between the separate firms constituting the fringe of small firms which in most markets fortunately coexist with the oligopoly of sizeable suppliers' (Bolton 1971, p. 49). They laid particular stress in this connection on the potential damage to small-firm competitive potential arising from the subjection of them and their trade associations, unnecessarily, to the rigours of Restrictive Trade Practices (RTP) legislation.

> We can see no reason on any grounds, economic or otherwise, for not permitting a group of small firms to combine in any way which they think desirable, subject of course to full disclosure to customers and others, to carry out any objective which would be permissible to a large firm, or the same small firms if they were merged. (Bolton 1971, p. 291)

As its boldest this boiled down to arguing that small-firm agreements should be leniently treated and exempted from reference to the RTP Court, unless they were substantial enough to account for a scale of activity or market share qualifying for a monopoly or merger reference. More modestly, their conclusion implied some form of *de minimis* provision for small firms or exemption from the legislation for certain kinds of small-firm agreements. They drew attention to the specific small-firm exemption provisions in contemporary EEC competition policy legislation and the possibility of exploiting the flexibility available in the UK by a generous use of that section of the Restrictive Practices Act permitting the Director General of Fair Trading to seek a direction from the Secretary of State not to send an agreement before the Court for adjudication.

In terms of competition policy the changes embodied in the Fair Trading Act 1973, the Competition Act 1980, and the Restrictive Trade Practices Acts of 1976 which, *inter alia*, extended the coverage of the legislation to include services, have gone some way to addressing the general problem of restraining anti-competitive behaviour raised in the Bolton Report. The most notable innovation perhaps being the introduction in the Competition Act of legislation to control anti-competitive practices by single firms, which were formerly outside the reach of the legislation where they did not involve registrable restrictive agreements or a statutory monopoly position. The 1973 Fair Trading Act also explicitly introduced both the desirability of maintaining 'effective competition' and a 'balanced distribution of industry and employment' as matters to be taken into account by the Monopolies and Mergers Commission in determining the effect of monopoly and merger upon the public interest, though neither of these matters is given a structural or specific small-firm connotation. The 1980 Competition Act was introduced following an extensive review of both Restrictive Trade Practices and Monopoly and Merger Legislation (HMSO 1979, 1978). The former addressed specifically a number of issues raised in Hughes (1978) which *inter alia* echoed the concerns of the Bolton Committee about the possibly inhibiting role which the Restrictive Trade Practices legislation might play in restricting desirable co-operative arrangements between small firms. The changes suggested as a result of the review excluded specific small-firm exemption and were not in any event incorporated in subsequent legislation. It is worth noting, however, that the block exemption provisions of the European Community legislation referred to by Bolton and discussed in the next section have, by contrast, been extended, most notably in the direction of schemes designed to promote research and development and technical change, and the Commission is at pains to emphasize its efforts to encourage small-firm performance in this way. The changes proposed in the 1988 Restrictive Practices consultative document (HMSO 1988a) would help move the UK further in this direction.

Competition policy in the EEC[15]

Competition policy in the European Community is governed by Articles 85 and 86 of the Treaty of Rome (and in the European Coal and Steel Community by Articles 60, 65 and 66(7) of the Treaty of Paris).

Articles 85 prohibits and declares null and void concerted practices, agreements between firms, and decisions by associations of firms which affect trade between member states and have as their object the restriction or distortion of competition within the EEC. Agreements of this sort, with a few exceptions, must be notified to the European Commission for investigation. After investigation exemption may be granted by the Commission where an agreement contributes to improved technical progress, or improved distribution and production of goods, and the purchaser or final consumer benefits 'fairly' from the resulting gains, in terms of lower prices or superior quality or availability of goods, and where a substantial element of the product market remains competitive and no restrictions are maintained which are not indispensable to achieving the benefits claimed. Judgment is administered with a final right of appeal to the Court of Justice.

In addition to individual exemption decisions, the Commission has emphasized that certain kinds of corporate behaviour can be regarded as beneficial even where competition is affected. Of particular relevance for small and medium-sized enterprises (SMEs) are the block exemption regulations arising from this position which gives blanket exemption from the prohibitions of Article 85(1). As set out in the Fifteenth Report on Competition Policy of the Commission of the European Communities these are of great importance to SMEs.

(a) no notification is required, thus avoiding time-consuming procedures:

(b) several block exemption regulations are of direct relevance for SMEs either because of the conditions for application (market share and turnover criteria) or because of the nature of the activity concerned, for example:

(i) non-reciprocal exclusive distribution agreements between competitors are only allowed if at least one of the parties has an annual turnover of less than 100 million ECU;

(ii) exclusive purchasing agreements normally involve SMEs (e.g. public houses and service stations); the block exemption regulation prevents the purchaser from being excessively bound to the supplier in terms of time and the range of products he buys;

(iii) motor vehicle distribution agreements: car dealers are usually SMEs; the regulation ensures that they are not made overly dependent on the supplier and affords greater freedom as to the dealer's use of spare parts and sales to other authorized dealers;

(iv) the patent licensing block exemption regulation both allows small firms (as licensees) to gain access to new technologies and also encourages the innovative activities of small firms, who (as licensors) can thus exploit their inventions throughout the Community via (bigger) licensees;

(v) the block exemption on specialization agreements,

which applies only where market share and turnover thresholds (20% and 500 million ECU) are not exceeded, was specially created to allow SMEs to improve their production processes and thereby strengthen their competitive position;

(vi) the research and development block exemption regulation provides that competing undertakings which together have a market share of less than 20% may engage in joint research and development and joint exploitation of the results; this criterion implies that nearly all agreements of this type involving SMEs will be covered. (EEC 1986)

Article 86 prohibits abuse by one or more undertakings of a dominant position within the Community or a substantial part of it in so far as it affects trade between member states. A dominant position is not well defined, unlike the specific definition provided in the UK legislation. Types of abuse prohibited include tie-in sales, price and other discrimination, limitations on output, etc. There is no notification procedure. The Commission depends on surveillance and complaints to enforce the legislation. As with Article 85 the findings of the Commission are subject to adjudication by the Court of Justice.

There are no specific provisions relating to merger. Article 86 has been applied to mergers as an abuse of a dominant position, though infrequently and without notable success. Draft proposals for a specific merger-control regulation have been circulating for a decade and a half without reaching a stage where implementation seems likely, largely because of differences in national approaches to the problem and potential clashes between national and community-wide control.

NOTES

1. No formal definition of a small firm is offered in this paper. Where the discussion in the text relates to specific size or types of firm the particular definition in use is indicated. This is particularly relevant where empirical evidence is discussed.

2. The analysis which follows is a very simplified exposition of the model of Downie (1958). The themes pursued there and in the richer Schumpeterian vision with which it is related are developed more formally in Metcalfe and Gibbons (1986), Levin (1978), Futia (1980), Flaherty (1980), Nelson and Winter (1977, 1978). This discussion abstracts from influences arising at the macroeconomic level. In times of

recession, for instance, there is a tendency for an increase in small-firm formation as entrepreneurial self-employment becomes an alternative to unemployment, with different industries being more or less affected, depending upon the industrial pattern of recession. (For a general discussion see Penrose (1959). For historical examples in the UK see Foreman-Peck (1985).) Contemporary changes in the share of small firms in total employment may also reflect this phenomenon and this must be borne in mind in interpreting recent trends in activity in the small-firm sector. (See for example the discussion in Storey and Johnson (1987a, 1987b).)

3. It is worth noting that even if there was no systematic tendency for firms of different sizes to experience different growth prospects, then concentration could increase simply because of the cumulative effect of the variance of growth rates across firms. This tendency may be offset if large firms grow systematically less fast than small ones or if there is a continuous net supply of small firms entering the market. See, for instance, Prais (1976); Hannah and Kay (1977).

4. These figures for manufacturing are based on movements in 3 or 5 firm employment concentration ratios at the three-digit level of disaggregation, and for retailing in terms of sales at a finer level of disaggregation.

5. Hay and Morris (1984) report unquoted companies as spending less on the acquisition of other companies as a percentage of total uses of funds than quoted companies (Figures 7.1 and 7.2, pp. 86–7). Representative data from their sample show for 1973 company acquisition activity at 7.4 per cent of total uses for quoted and 4.5 per cent for non-quoted companies. For 1976 in the low merger activity period, the figures were 3.3 per cent and 1.4 per cent respectively. This data however excludes acquisitions financed by new issues.

6. Mergers involving the acquisition of domestic manufacturing concerns by overseas producers may also be prohibited under powers given to the Secretary of State in Part II of the Industry Act 1975 who may also intervene by compulsory acquisition of a threatened domestic concern. The discussion of competition policy prior to 1980 in this Appendix draws upon Hughes (1978), HMSO (1979).

7. Certain broad categories of agreement are exempt from requirements to register. These have included at various times:

(i) (Since 1969) agreements certified by the Secretary of State for Prices and Consumer Protection as being needed for a project of substantial importance to the national economy, or concerned with promoting industrial efficiency, or to create or improve productive capacity, and on balance expedient in the national interest. Such exemptions are made for limited periods, but are renewable. They must contain no registrable restrictions or information provisions other than those needed for the project in question.

(ii) Certain government-based schemes for price reduction or limitation.

(iii) Normal contracts of sale from one party to the other party.

(iv) Agreements concerning patents and trade marks, although agreements among three or more parties to pool patents or licences, which agreements also contain restrictions, are registrable (since 1973).

(v) Agreements relating solely to exports or to operations abroad but details of such agreements must be notified to the DGFT.

(vi) Agreements authorized under European Coal and Steel Community rules.

(vii) Industry-wide rationalization schemes, certified by the Secretary of State, for the elimination of redundant capacity.

8. In contrast, the Resale Prices Act does not involve registration but prohibits individual and collective resale price maintenance as aspects of business behaviour and makes it unlawful to use such practices as refusal to supply, to introduce or reinforce them. To be exempt from the prohibition a class of goods must establish before the Restrictive Trade Practices Court that there are net benefits to the public arising from the avoidance of reductions in the quality and range of goods available; the number of retail outlets; higher prices; services necessarily provided with the goods; damage to the health of the public.

9. The question of registrability itself may be challenged in a separate action in the Restrictive Practices Court.

10. In addition, the DGFT need not refer if the agreements are determined (i.e. terminated or expired or where restrictions have been removed by negotiation) or he feels it appropriate in the light of European Community provisions.

11. Before 1973, the legislations make no reference to competition being desirable *per se*.

12. The Commission may also recommend, and the Secretary of State accept the recommendation, that the monopoly in question should be broken up.

13. EEC as well as UK competition policy is concerned with the abuse, or the undesirable effects, of a dominant position rather than a condemnation of particular firm scale or market structure – indeed, the potential benefits of scale economies are well recognized in both sets of policy. The principal difference between the two policies is in what would be counted as abuse – in the EEC it is where inter-state trade is affected, in the UK it is where performance (from a national interest viewpoint) is affected. In the UK investigation to ascertain whether a monopoly exists and, if so, how it has behaved, is the norm. In the EEC investigation by the Commission is more usual in connection with an already-suspected abuse.

14. Both the Director General's investigatory powers and his powers of referral to the Monopolies and Mergers Commission are subject to veto by the Secretary of State.

15. This section is based on the Commission of the European Communities (1986); HMSO (1979); Swann (1983).

REFERENCES

Bolton (1971) *Small Firms: Report of the Committee of Inquiry on Small Firms*, London: HMSO.

Bolton (1972) *A Postal Questionnaire Survey of Small Firms' Non Financial Data*, Research Report No 17, London: HMSO.

Boswell, J. (1972) *The Rise and Decline of Small Firms*, London: Allen & Unwin.

Burns, T. and Stalker, G.M. (1961) *The Management of Innovation*, London: Tavistock.

Butters, J.K., Lintner, J., and Cary, W.L. (1951) *The Effects of Taxation on Corporate Mergers*, Cambridge, Mass.: Harvard University Press.

Clarke, R. (1985) *Industrial Economics*, London.

Commission for the European Communities (1986) *Fifteenth Report on Competition Policy*, Brussels.

Cosh, A.D., Hughes, A., and Singh, A. (1980) 'The causes and effects of takeovers in the UK', in D.C. Mueller (ed.) (1980) op. cit.

Cowling, *et al.* (1980) *Mergers and Economic Performance*, Cambridge: Cambridge University Press.

Coyne, J. and Wright, M. (1986) *Management Buyouts*, London: Croom Helm.

Cyert, R.M. and George, K.D. (1969) 'Competition, growth, and efficiency', *Economic Journal* LXXIX, March: 23–41.

Davies, J.R. and Kuehn, D.A. (1977) 'An investigation into the effectiveness of a capital market sanction on poor performance' in Jacquemin, A.P. and De Jong, H.W. (eds), *Welfare Aspects of Industrial Markets*, Leiden: Martinus Neijhoff.

Downie, J. (1958) *The Competitive Process*, London: Duckworth.

EEC (1986) *Fifteenth Report on Competition Policy*, Brussels.

Flaherty, M.T. (1980) 'Industry structure and cost reducing investment', *Econometrica* 48: 187–209.

Foreman-Peck, J.S. (1985) 'Seedcorn or chaff? New firm formation and the performance of the interwar economy', *Economic History Review*, August, 402–22.

Freeman, C. (1982) *The Economics of Industrial Innovation*, London: Frances Pinter.

Futia, C.A. (1980) 'Schumpeterian competition', *Quarterly Journal of Economics* 94: 675–95.

Gallagher, C.C. and Doyle, J.R. (1986) *Job Generation and Loss by Firm Size in the UK*, Research Report No 5, Department of Industrial Management, University of Newcastle-upon-Tyne.

Ganguly, P. (1982) 'Small firms survey: the international scene', *British Business* 19 Nov.: 486–91.

Grinyer, P.H. and Spender, J.C. (1979) *Turnaround: The Fall and Rise of the Newton Chambers Group*, London: Associated Business Press.

Hannah, L. and Kay, J.A. (1977) *Concentration in Modern Industry*, London: Macmillan.

Hart, P. and Clarke, R. (1980) *Concentration in British Industry 1935–75*, Cambridge: Cambridge University Press.

Hart, P.E. (1987) 'Small firms and jobs', *National Institute Economic Review*, August, pp. 60–6.

Hay, D.A. and Morris, D.J. (1984) *Unquoted Companies*, London: Macmillan.

HMSO (1978) *A Review of Monopolies and Mergers Policy*, London.

HMSO (1979) *A Review of Restrictive Trade Practices Policy*, London.

HMSO (1985) *Competition in Retailing*, London.

HMSO (1988a) *Review of Restrictive Trade Practices Policy: A Consultative Document*, London.

HMSO (1988b) *Mergers Policy: A Department of Trade and Industry Paper on the Policy and Procedures of Merger Control*, London.

Hill, C.W.L. (1984) 'Profile of a conglomerate takeover: BTR and Thomas Tilling', *Journal of General Management*, Winter.

Hill, C.W.L. and Pickering, J. (1986) 'Divisionalisation, decentralisation and performance of large UK companies', *Journal of Management Studies* 27.

Hornby, D. (1986) 'Can we teach ourselves to change?', *Royal Bank of Scotland Review*, September.

Hughes, A. (1978) 'Competition policy and economic performance in the UK' in NEDO, *Competition Policy*, London: HMSO.

Hughes, A. and Kumar, M.S. (1984a) 'Recent trends in aggregate concentration in the UK economy', *Cambridge Journal of Economics*, September.

Hughes, A. and Kumar, M.S. (1984b) 'Recent trends in aggregate concentration in the UK economy revised estimates', *Cambridge Journal of Economics*, December.

Hughes, A. (1989) 'The impact of merger: a survey of empirical evidence for the UK', in J. Fairburn and J.A. Kay (eds), *Merger and Merger Policy*, Oxford University Press (forthcoming).

Kitching, J. (1967) 'Why do mergers miscarry?', *Harvard Business Review*, November–December.

Kitching, J. (1974) 'Why acquisitions are abortive', *Management Today*.

Kuehn, D.A. (1975) *Takeovers and the Theory of the Firm*, London: Macmillan.

Kumar, M.S. (1984) *Growth Acquisition and Investment*, Cambridge: Cambridge University Press.

Levin, R.C. (1978) 'Technical change, barriers to entry and market structure', *Economica* 45: 347–61.

Lowe, J. and Crawford, N. (1984) *Innovation and Technology Transfer for the Growing Firm*, Oxford: Pergamon.

McEachern, W.A. and Romeo, A. (1978) 'Stockholder control, uncertainty and the allocation of resources to research and development', *Journal of Industrial Economics* XXVI: 135–62.

Meeks, G. (1977) *Disappointing Marriage: A Study of the Gains from Merger*, Cambridge: Cambridge University Press.

Merret Cyriax Associates (1971) *Dynamics of Small Firms*, Research Report No 12, Committee of Enquiry on Small Firms, London: HMSO.

Metcalfe, J.S. and Gibbons, M. (1986) 'Technological variety and the process of competition', *Economie Appliquée* tome XXXIX, no. 3, 493–520.

Moos, S. (1971) *Aspects of Monopoly and Restrictive Practices Legislation in Relation to Small Firms*, Research Report No 13, Committee of Enquiry on Small Firms, London: HMSO.

Mueller, D.C. (1980) *The Determinants and Effects of Mergers*, Cambridge, Mass.: Oelgeschlaeger Gunn and Hain.

Mueller, D.C. (1986) *Profits in the Long Run*, Cambridge: Cambridge University Press.

Nelson, R.L. and Winter, S.G. (1977) 'Dynamic competition and technical progress', in B. Balassa and R.R. Nelson (eds), *Economic Progress and Values and Public Policy: Essays in Honour of William Fellner*, Amsterdam: North Holland.

Nelson, R.L. and Winter, S.G. (1978) 'Forces generating and limiting concentration under Schumpeterian competition', *Bell Journal of Economics* 9: 524–48.

OECD (1984) *Merger Policy and Recent Trends in Mergers*, Paris: OECD.

OECD (1986) *Annual Reports on Competition Policy in Member States*, Paris: OECD.

Office of Fair Trading (1980) *Annual Report of the Director General of the Office of Fair Trading*, London: HMSO.

Office of Fair Trading (1985a) *Annual Report of the Director General of the Office of Fair Trading*, London: HMSO.

Office of Fair Trading (1985b) *Competition in Retailing*, London: HMSO.

Ordover, J.A. and Willig, R.D. (1985) 'Antitrust for high-technology industries: assessing research, joint ventures, and mergers', *Journal of Law and Economics* XXVIII, May.

Pavitt, K. and Wald, S. (1971) *The Conditions for Success in Technological Innovation*, Paris: OECD.

Peach, L.H. and Hargreaves, J. (1976) 'Social responsibility: the investment that pays off', *Personnel Management* 8 (6).

Penrose, E.T. (1959) *The Theory of the Growth of the Firm*, London: Oxford.

Porter, M. (1980) *Competitive Strategy*, New York: Free Press.

Prais, S.J. (1976) *The Evolution of Giant Firms in the United Kingdom*, Cambridge: Cambridge University Press.

Rhoades, S.A. (1983) *Power, Empire Building and Mergers*, Lexington, Mass.: D.C. Heath and Co.

Rosenberg, N. (ed.) (1973) *The Economics of Technological Change*, Harmondsworth: Penguin.

Samuels, J.M. (1971) 'The success or failure of mergers and takeovers', *Journal of Business Policy*, Spring.

Samuels, J.M. and Chesher, A.D. (1972) 'Growth, survival and the size of companies 1960–69', in Cowling, K. (ed.), *Market Structure and Corporate Behaviour*, London: Gray Mills.

Sargent, V. (1981) *Large Firms and Small Firms: A Review of Current Activities*, London: London Enterprise Agency.

Scherer, F.M. and Ravenscraft, D. (1984) 'Growth by diversification: entrepreneurial behaviour in large-scale United States enterprise', *Zeitschrift fur National Okonomie*, Supplement No 4.

171

Scherer, F.M. (1980) *Industrial Market Structure and Economic Performance*, Chicago: Rand McNally.

Shaw, R.W. and Simpson, P. (1986) 'The persistence of monopoly: an investigation of the effectiveness of the UK Monopolies Commission', *Journal of Industrial Economics*, June.

Singh, A. (1975) 'Takeovers, economic natural selection and the theory of the firm evidence from postwar UK experience', *Economic Journal*, September.

Storey, D.J. (ed.) (1983) *The Small Firm*, Beckenham: Croom Helm.

Storey, D.J. and Johnson, S. (1987a) *Are Small Firms the Answer to Unemployment?*, London: Employment Institute.

Storey, D.J. and Johnson, S. (1987b) *Job Generation and Labour Market Change*, London: Macmillan.

Swann, D. (1983) *Competition and Industrial Policy in the European Community*, London: Methuen.

Utton, M.A. (1972) 'Mergers and the growth of large firms', *Oxford Bulletin of Economics and Statistics*, May.

Utton, M.A. (1986) *Profits and the Stability of Monopoly*, Cambridge: Cambridge University Press.

White, L.J. (1982) 'The determinants of the relative importance of small business', *Review of Economics and Statistics*, February.

Williamson, O.E. (1970) *Corporate Control and Business Behaviour*, Englewood Cliffs, N.J.: Prentice-Hall.

Williamson, O.E. (1975) *Markets and Hierarchies: Analysis and Anti-Trust Implications*, New York: Free Press.

Williamson, O.E. (1985) *The Economic Institutions of Capitalism*, New York: Free Press.

Worcester, D.A. (1957) 'Why "dominant" firms decline', *Journal of Political Economy*, August, 338–47.

Wright, M. and Coyne, J. (1985) *Management Buy Outs*, London: Croom Helm.

8

Barriers to Growth: The Effects of Market Structure

John McGee

INTRODUCTION

There has been a long history of concern with the 'small' firm, its ability to survive against large competitors, its role in sparking innovation and creating change, and latterly in being the prime source of new employment. However, there has also been an even more powerful lobby over the years extolling the virtues of the large firm as the engine room of economic progress and the natural exploiters of various scale economies.

The immediate difficulty in analysing small firms faced by the Bolton Committee of Inquiry in 1969 was the almost complete absence of research information on the small-firm sector at that time, coupled with a lack of definition of what was meant by the term 'small firm'. According to Stanworth *et al.* (1982): 'the numerical picture of the small enterprise in Britain in 1981 appears no clearer . . . in some respects it is becoming less clear'.

Discussions of the statistics on small firms are available elsewhere (e.g. Ganguly 1985), and there has been a wealth of research (for summaries see Levicki 1984, Stanworth *et al.* 1982). The principal difficulty lies with the concept of the 'small firm', the way it is operationalized in empirical research and the implications this carries (if any) for policy making in government. Bolton inspired a set of definitions that revolved around the idea of small size (whether in absolute or relative terms), and personal risks undertaken by owner-managers. Many research studies use absolute size measures (e.g. in manufacturing a small firm has less than 200 employees, in construction it has less than 25 employees (Bolton 1971)). The importance of firms in economic analysis depends also on measures relative to market size in order to understand and allow for factors which limit the size of the firm. According to Bannock (1981):

> A small firm is one that has only a small share of its market, is managed in a personalized way by its owners . . . and not though the medium of an elaborate management structure and which is not sufficiently large to have access to the capital market for the public issue or placing of securities.

This excludes, therefore, subsidiaries of larger companies. The Bolton Committee estimated that according to its own definitions small firms employed about 25 per cent of the working population in the UK and accounted for some 20 per cent of GDP. While their importance may have declined somewhat in the 1980s, the economic significance of the 'small firm' is still very high and is thought to be higher still in other countries (Ganguly 1985).

However, the arbitrariness of statistical definitions gives cause for concern. In a market economy the unit of economic activity is a continuum without clear break points. The appropriate unit of analysis is either the industry, the market, or the firm itself, and the focus for investigation is the nature of competitive activity and its implications for resource allocation, progressiveness, and national competitiveness. The focus of attention is the interaction between competitors and in some circumstances the role of the small firms *vis-à-vis* their larger competitors is of prime interest. Small, in terms of competition, is a purely relative concept. In some circumstances competitors that are large in absolute (Bolton) terms regard themselves as 'small' (or competitively disadvantaged) relative to the market leaders. Following this theme there is a growing strategic management literature which focuses on low market share business.

If we turn our attenion to the dynamics of an industry and its pattern of evolution, our concern is with the sources of invention and innovation and the diffusion of change throughout an industry. Change may be diffused through inter-firm channels (in which we might include merger activity) and by the organic growth of firms (intra-firm channels). In the former case we are concerned with the role of the small(er) firm in provoking change – but, like the male that fertilizes the queen bee, does it have to die in the process? Industries marked by maturity of products, markets, and technologies generally have stable firm size distributions and organic growth in excess of natural market growth is not common. Changes in relative sizes of firms is usually associated with changes and shifts in the underlying parameters, sometimes of the 'shift' type (e.g., the advent of Japanese automakers into hitherto fairly stable US and European markets), probably more often of the evolutionary, new technology and new market genus in which the progenitors of change are firms which have grown from nothing to impressive size (e.g., IBM, Xerox, Polaroid). In this instance, we are concerned with the problems of growth at all stages and, *inter alia*, with the problems of 'start-up' and 'development'. It is quite possible that the significance of (absolutely) small firms lies in their presence as a competitive spur and as a prompter of change, but not necessarily in their ability to transform an industry by virtue of their own organic growth. It is, however, much more likely that the pattern of industry evolution and the growth paths of firms are highly significant issues where markets and technologies are themselves novel and innovatory.

On *a priori* grounds such as these it would be sensible to hypothesize that issues of efficiency (the competitive spur) and issues of growth are related to the underlying product market characteristics and that the outcomes in terms of the size, significance, and conduct of the small-firm sector will vary accordingly.

After this concern with the nature of the subject, we will outline the traditional characteristics of market structure and the issues for small firms. We will then discuss the meaning of 'competitive advantage' for the small firm and the implications for firm strategies and the management process. A context of innovating firms in young developing markets will be assumed but much of the discussion is applicable to firms in a wide range of industry environments. The hypothesis advanced is that small firms in these circumstances are more disadvantaged by their own inability to take advantage of market opportunities than by the structural characteristics of these markets and the inherent power of existing competitors. This argument leaves open the possibility that other environmental characteristics such as the tax structure, capital markets, and labour markets might differentially penalize the smaller firm.

MARKET STRUCTURE

The characteristics of market structure can be summarized under headings of:

  (i) Cost conditions
 (ii) Market characteristics
(iii) Vertical market structures
(iv) Concentration

These lead to propositions about the nature of competitive rivalry in the industry.

Cost conditions

Cost differences between firms can arise either as absolute cost advantages or as cost advantages arising from size. Absolute cost advantages refer to factor cost differences arising from access to cheap labour, favourable raw materials supply or cheap capital. These are of minor interest here whereas advantages arising from superior size are at the centre of the small–large firm debate. The normal proposition holds that the existence of static and/or dynamic economies of scale confers cost advantages upon the largest firms eroded only by fundamental changes in the underlying market and technological conditions. Thus economies of scale arising from division of labour and capital intensity lead to increases in concentration and to sustainable cost advantages of the largest firms. The White Paper introducing the Industrial Reorganization Corporation argues:

> The need for more concentration and rationalization to promote greater efficiency and international competitiveness of British Industry . . . is now widely recognized . . . . Many of the production units in this country are small by comparison with the most successful companies in international trade . . . . In some sectors the typical company in Britain is too small to undertake long production runs; to take advantage of economies of scale; undertake effective research and development; to support specialist departments for design and marketing; to install the most modern equipment; or to attract the best qualified management. (HMSO 1966)

176

The review of competition policy (HMSO 1978) summarizes the position:

> Increasing firm size will be encouraged by economies of scale. These arise where the technology of production brings about falling costs per unit of output with an increasing rate of production up to the 'minimum efficient plant size' – the size of plant beyond which cost savings become small. Estimates of minimum efficient plant size have been as high as over 50 per cent of UK production for goods such as electric motors or tractors down to less than 1 per cent for shoes or bricks. These technical economies of scale may be offset by diseconomies which arise from the greater likelihood of strikes, difficulties of communication and the management problems associated with increasing plant size. There may, in addition, be economies of scale at the firm level due to the spreading of overheads, the use of common facilities and financial savings but these too may be offset by managerial diseconomies. Plant and firm level economies of scale help to explain the tendency for capital-intensive and mass-consumption goods industries to be highly concentrated.

The idea that some minimum efficient size is required comes clearly through these and many other sources. Subsequent work (e.g. Prais 1981) distinguishes between technical economies of scale at the plant level and the growth of firms in aggregate. Utton (in Levicki 1984) summarizes an interesting literature: 'Technical efficiency, therefore, seems to have played little or no part in the growth of aggregate concentration.' By technical efficiency he means technical economies of scale.

Furthermore, he suggests that production costs are in practice fairly insensitive to substantial variations in (planned) output around the minimum efficient plant size. He concludes, somewhat controversially, that the cost penalties for small plants (< 200 people) need not be very large.

Advantages from technical economies of scale are clearly only obtainable where the size of market permits. Scherer et al. (1975) in examining the economies of multi-plant operation explain much of the variance between minimum efficient plant sizes and actual size in terms of market size, transport costs, and the sensitivity of unit costs to planned volumes at non-optimal scales.

The theme that technological economies of scale combined with sufficient size of markets permits larger plants and higher concentration ratios is clearly supported by the evidence for some markets. It follows that in these markets the consequences of concentration can be beneficial from a resource allocation point of view. The review of competition policy (HMSO 1978) singles out cars, turbo-generators, and small electric motors as sectors where the largest UK plants are too small to enjoy the full benefits of economies of scale. However, it does not explain the overall increase in size of *firms*. According to the review of competition policy:

> There may be advantages from greater concentration at the firm level where scale economies and learning effects also operate. It may enable more effective financial and marketing operations, especially in foreign markets. Or the costs of innovation in areas like petroleum and chemicals can be such that a high level of concentration is necessary if the benefits of new and improved technology are to be harnessed. Indeed, a merger may be the only effective way of injecting improved technology or better management into a sector.

Against the advantages of plant and firm size are the arguments which assert that internal inefficiencies arise from size, especially where the exercise of market power is in the direction of tolerating inefficiency rather than maximizing profits. The weaker form of the argument, namely that size *per se* creates inefficiencies, depends critically on notions of diseconomies of scale (e.g., in co-ordinating complex activities on large sites). Without such diseconomies, inefficiencies would be effectively contained by competitive discipline in the market-place.

The correlation between high market share and profitability has received both empirical and theoretical support (Boston Consulting Group 1974; Gale 1972; Imel and Helmberger 1971; PIMS 1977; Shepherd 1972). On this basis, many have concluded that low market share firms occupy very difficult positions. As a very large number, if not most, businesses have low shares, this has rather uncomfortable implications that nothing much can be done as only a few will have the ability or the luck to reposition themselves. These conclusions have been challenged by a number of writers (Hamermesh *et al.* 1978; Woo and Cooper 1981; Woo and Cooper 1985) who have emphasized the range of options available to the small firms. Hamermesh *et al.* suggest four basic strategies:

(i) Creative market segmentation
(ii) Good leadership
(iii) Controlled growth
(iv) Efficient use of R&D resources

Woo and Cooper (1981) observed that 'effective' low-share businesses can be found in industries with high degrees of stability within which they focused on particular competitive variables (usually high-quality products). Their 1985 study concentrated on the extent to which corporate characteristics contribute towards the performance of low-share subsidiaries – a proposition beyond the scope of this chapter.

The general conclusion is that size is not a decisive consideration. Plant and firm size effects do exist. Their pervasiveness, their salience, and the ability of firms to secure the cost advantages have been much debated. Conversely, there is a stream of research which suggests that alternative strategies for small firms do exist.

Market characteristics

Although economies of scale leading to cost disadvantages for small firms are the obvious area for concern, behind them lie a number of issues relating to the size and segmentation of markets. Market size is a necessary condition for achieving economies of scale, in particular, the existence of broad, homogeneous markets susceptible to standardized products. Market evolution is rarely still, however, and markets do tend to become more heterogeneous over time, evolving into progressively finer segments as buyer tastes and technological opportunities change. Some recent evidence for this is available on automobiles, knitwear, and domestic appliances in Europe (Baden Fuller 1982). The significance of such segmentation lies in the differences in the assets and the resources required to meet buyer requirements in different segments. There can be significant 'mobility barriers' (McGee and Thomas 1986) between segments requiring risky investments in new assets in order to enter new market segments. The supplying industry in these circumstances becomes partitioned like the market into segments or 'strategic groups'. Some companies are positioned to deliver into several segments, others specialize in particular segments. The mode of competition can shift from pure price supported by cost advantage to provision of quality, service, and so on – the idea of 'differentiation'.

Just as division of labour is limited by market size, the converse is also true, heterogeneity of the market permits market segmentation and the use of product differentiation to create 'specialist' or 'niche' strategies by firms. The mobility barriers which enforce the segmentation stem from a variety of causes. Transport costs are the traditional segmentors of spatially separated markets. Patents and R&D create privileged access to segments by virtue of their firm-specific character. Some theories of industry evolution and industry life-style chart the progression from unified broad markets to increasingly narrower specialized segment structures. The broad market is susceptible to one key competitive advantage (e.g. patent, or cost position). Segmented and specialized markets require 'positioning' of assets against specific buying criteria in such a way as to hinder competition mobility between segments. Broad segmentation often decays into much finer segments or niches between which mobility barriers are much lower. The Bolton Committee observed:

> Limited markets do not necessarily produce small firms as a limited market can be supplied by a large firm supplying a number of markets. Nevertheless, limited markets are a major source of business strength. Such markets place a constraint on the size of the firm only when there are advantages of specialization. Consequently, small firms tend to specialize in limited markets when the product is sufficiently differentiated to make its combination with other products difficult.
>
> (Davies and Kelly 1972)

The conventional recommendation to a small firm is therefore to concentrate on relatively narrow markets which it can serve distinctively well. The necessary condition for survival, therefore, is the existence of segmented and protectable markets. However, the growth of segments attracts entry. IBM are reputed (McGee *et al.* 1986) to consider entry to any segment of the IT industry whose worldwide revenues exceed $500m. Thus, segments become of interest to large firms as their size offers opportunities to defray entry costs. The more substantial the entry costs, the bigger must be the prize. Conversely, the position of the large company in a broad market can be eroded away by smaller companies focusing on pieces of the industry. This is normally an

Table 8.1: Strategies for small-share competitors in mature industries. (Source: Thomas and Gardner, 1985, p. 455)

Reference	Marketing strategy recommendations	Other strategic recommendations
Hamermesh *et al.* (1978)	Seek creative segmentation	Maintain top-quality management Manage controlled growth Spend efficiently on R&D
Woo and Cooper (1979)	Avoid head-to-head competition Stress just one market differentiating variable Don't have equal product-line breadth as competitors Provide relatively high quality for moderate price (good value)	
Buzzell and Wiersema (1981)	Focus on smaller, narrowed segments less influenced by scale (i.e. service, captive, regional, etc.) and where product redesign possible Keep marketing expenses low Emphasize quality Avoid aggressive competitors	
Hall (1980)	Provide highly differentiated product	Have lowest costs
Hamermesh and Silk (1979)	Select growth segments Provide high-quality products Provide innovative products	Maintain efficient production and distribution
Leavitt (1980)	Differentiate product-service offerings	
Hofer and Davoust (1977)	Specialize in offerings Seek market niches Invest in growth segments Prune product lines	Consider exit Don't rock the boat Minimize investment
Ward and Stasch (1980b)	Provide meaningful and significant competitive differences Attack lethargic competitors	
Strategic Planning Institute (1979)	Select defensible segments Have broader or narrower product line than competition Develop high-quality differentiation Introduce relatively more new products	Minimize R&D
Boston Consulting Group (1968)	Focus on differentiated, protected niches Invest aggressively in fast growth segments	Combined related businesses Change production or distribution 'economics' in industry

181

indication of the wearing out of the original competitive advantage as the industry breaks into segments (see Ghazanfar 1984; McGee, Ghazanfar and Thomas 1986). The erosion of Birds Eye's dominant position in the frozen food industry and the growth of smaller specialist companies is a classic example (Grant 1985).

The challenge for small firms is to serve (relatively) narrow markets distinctively well – 'specialization' – with an approach that is not readily replicated by larger competitors partly because of the distinctiveness of the small firm's approach, and partly because the segment is not sufficiently large to warrant attention. Specialization strategies require a continuous and concerted effort to differentiate in terms of, for example, product performance, customer service and support, and custom-made products. From the limited resource base of the small firm, differentiation is usually based on highly specific factors. Fast growth of individual segments can be a mixed blessing by attracting new entrants. Diversification by small firms into adjacent product market segments can be an effective way of avoiding large competitors but at the cost of further strain on normally slender technical and managerial capabilities (see below).

Stasch and Ward (1985) have summarized the literature on strategies for small-share competitors (see Table 8.1). This literature suggests two basic strategies:

(i) Invest selectively in fast growth markets; and/or
(ii) Seek and develop specialized niches with a highly differential offering.

This highlights the importance of *marketing* and product market positioning in creating strategic advantage as opposed to other issues such as cost position, investment, and R&D.

Vertical market structures

Industry structure analysis now pays a lot of attention to the vertical structure of markets. For the firm this means assessing its bargaining power with suppliers and with customers. Bargaining power affects key variables such as price, availability of product, access to markets, and inventories. Small firms can effectively lose their independence as large buyers tie-in their suppliers through technical assistance, trade credit, long-term contracts and so on. Some small suppliers may prosper on this quasi-vertically integrated structure but they grow and prosper as satellites of the larger buyer, not through their own strength and independence.

The Bolton Committee pointed out that over a third of small manufacturers sell more than 25 per cent of their output to one customer, this dependency decreasing with size of firm (Davies and Kelly 1972). NEDC observed in its evidence to Bolton that small firms frequently act as the provider of a reservoir of surplus capacity (NEDC 1970). Mayer observed in 1947 that the small manufacturer is *de facto* the manager of a branch plant (Mayer 1947). Vertical market power can thus result in small firms being strategically *dependent* – their survival rests on how large firms choose to exercise control over the vertical structure.

Research at the London Business School (Slatter 1987) suggests that small 'high-technology' firms have difficulty dealing with large suppliers. Microelectronic companies very often have to buy from overseas suppliers who require long lead times (20–25 weeks). For small firms in volatile markets, this requires risking inventory commitment as well as the burden of foreign exchange risk. Small firms dealing with large licensors often find it difficult to find the front-end cash payments for licences. Similarly, large suppliers extract potential rents from downstream markets by controlling price and/or suppliers of key components (e.g. semi-custom chips).

The essential issues were argued by Galbraith:

> The long trend towards concentration of industrial enterprise in the hands of relatively few firms has brought into existence not only strong sellers . . . but also strong buyers. . . . Power on one side of the market creates both the need for, and prospect of, reward, to the exercise of countervailing power from the other side. (Galbraith 1957)

The passage of time has if anything, reinforced this theme. Aggregate concentration has increased (Bannock 1984; Utton 1984), discriminatory buying power has been the subject of much attention (Office of Fair Trading 1985), and supplying industries have responded by mergers and alliances to rectify the balance of bargaining power.

Lustgarten (1975) examined the effect of buyer and seller concentration on price-cost margins. He found that buyer concentration

Figure 8.1: Joint effect of buyer power and seller power

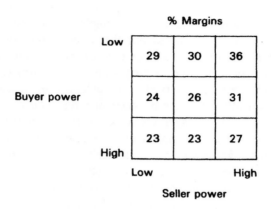

Source: Adapted from Fitzroy (1985).

was associated with seller concentration, consistent with Galbraith's thesis. Also he found that buyer concentration was negatively correlated with seller price-cost margins, consistent with the bargaining power hypotheses. Fitzroy (1985) used the PIMS data base to explore the interaction of buyer power and seller power on seller profitability (see Figure 8.1). Two of his results are of particular interest. The first confirms the obvious proposition that where there is low buyer power, sellers find it easier to exercise the power they possess. On the other hand, if buyer power is higher, sellers find it difficult to exercise their power. Figure 8.1 illustrates this, measuring buyer power by purchase size, seller power as the inverse of the Herfindahl index and the outcome as average margins.

The second result concerns the effect of market share on this relationship. According to Fitzroy:

> While seller power as a market parameter typically helps the margins of suppliers it does not necessarily help all competitors in the market place equally. Small competitors cannot take advantage of this seemingly higher concentrated market.

The position of the small firm is particularly disadvantaged when it has no distinctiveness of its own. When the provision of standardized goods at relatively low prices is the key to success then the small firm is vulnerable both to its larger competitors as well as to large buyers. Similarly, the small firm whose success is dependent on competitive advantage which arises from the distinctiveness of its suppliers' components is vulnerable to these suppliers. Lack of bargaining power is primarily a function of relative size when size and unit cost are related somewhere in the chain of supply to the final customer. Degrees of strategic freedom for the small firm are usually associated with distinctiveness and differentiation. Small firms acting as mere channels and conduits are clearly vulnerable.

Concentration

The general concern of public policy makers is the avoidance of monopoly and the exercise of market power. Concentration is regarded as an important indicator of the centralization of economic activity and power within individual markets and in the economy as a whole. A discussion of measures of concentration is available in Aaronovitch and Sawyer (1975) and of their desirable properties in Hannah and Kay (1977). Propositions about the relationship between concentration and market size are noted in Sawyer (1981). The differences between plant concentration levels (which should be technologically determined) and firm concentration levels have been discussed by many authors. The rise in the aggregate level of concentration and the increase in diversification of large firms (at least up to the end of the 1970s) have also been widely discussed. Utton (1984), for example, debates whether the large diversified firm gains advantage from its wider boundaries. The empirical evidence is sparse (Utton 1984) but there is an emerging school of thought (Rumelt 1974; Salter and Weinhold 1979; Meeks 1977) that unrelated diversifiers do not gain advantage. But see Leontiades (1986) for a different view. From there it is not far to the proposition that the urge to merge is somewhat less than rational and that mergers frequently miscarry (Kitching 1967; Meeks 1977).

This has two points of significance for the small firm. The first is that 'undisciplined' takeover activity creates units whose size is unrelated to performance, and cultivates a 'corporate state' ethos in which the political power of large companies and trade unions mutually foster each other and thereby bias the system against the

185

interest of small firms (Bannock 1981). These effects are argued to be subtle but progressive in their operation but the empirical evidence as to their extent and significance is indirect. For the small firm, the central issue is the control of mergers perhaps by shifting the onus of proof onto the acquiring company to show benefit. The public interest is difficult to define with clarity but as Bannock argues, if large mergers were banned outright it is doubtful that much would be lost.

The 1980s have seen a more critical view of the diversified firm, and anecdotal evidence suggests that firms are reducing their span of interests and focusing more carefully on their 'core' businesses. Enlightened self-interest may well have effects such as this but demerger initiatives could greatly accelerate this process.

The second major concern for the smaller firm is the implications for competitive behaviour of large, diversified competitors, Utton summarizes the 'deep pocket' and the 'mutual forbearance' arguments. The former suggests that rents from the exercise of market power in some businesses can be used to subsidize entry into new businesses, the costs of which will then be recouped after the expulsion of weaker and/or smaller rivals by exercising market power again. This version of the predatory pricing argument depends on strong assumptions about the ability to exercise market power in at least one 'core' business and in at least one 'new' business, both of which require significant and durable entry barriers. This argument in somewhat weaker form is used to describe the sequential building of market positions in different parts of the world. Surplus cash flow from the domestic base is used (see Prahalad and Hamel 1985) to finance entry into new markets. This variant of 'deep pocket' probably owes as much to supposed imperfections in capital markets as to the exercise of market power.

The 'mutual forbearance' argument suggests that conglomerate competitors adopt a policy of live and let live rather than risk destabilizing the entire structure of conglomerate relationships. According to Edwards (1964):

> The great conglomerates may come to have recognized spheres of influence and may hesitate to fight local wars vigorously because the prospects of local gain are not worth the risk of general warfare.

Porter (1985) analyses multipoint competition from the point of view of 'stabilizing factors' and 'focal points' (a market share concept) around which competitive activity will stabilize. He observes that: 'competitor interrelationships are numerous and have increased significantly over time, particularly during the 1960s and 1970s'.

Utton (1984) draws up a warning scenario:

The scope for individual initiatives by medium and small firms is continually restricted . . . because the prospects for smaller companies of successfully entering industries not only dominated by market leaders which are among the country's largest companies but also where a number of subsidiaries of other massive companies are active. In this way entry to different industries may pass largely into the hands of a relatively small group of giants . . . the prospect may then be one of an increasingly inflexible and sluggish industrial sector with greatly diminished opportunities for smaller firms.

The implications of this for small firms are unclear. Arguments about quasi-oligopolistic collusion founder on the rocks of competition: small and medium-sized firms can undercut and erode price leadership policies. Pre-emption of the market by large firms is also unconvincing if there is no additional premise to explain how the larger firm can obtain competitive advantage or market power. The large, inefficient firm is a source of joy to the small firm. The relevant concern with large diversified firms is the extent to which the parent can contribute to the competitive advantage of the acquired subsidiary (Woo and Cooper 1985; and see also Salter and Weinhold 1979; and Leontiades 1986). If the acquisition is of conglomerate style, then the presumption is that synergies are absent or minimal. If it is a related diversification then synergies are not only possible but, from a resource allocation viewpoint, they are welcomed.

By itself, unrelated diversification confers no advantages on the conglomerate at least in terms of the ability to compete in the market-place. To the extent that some elements of market power are conferred via absolute cost advantages arising for example from imperfect capital markets or from the tax system, then there is concern for the small competitors. But if the exercise of market power and the user of anti-competitive tactics can be controlled, then there is no reason to suppose that large diversified firms enjoy 'unfair' advantages. However, some might argue that a

187

suitably vigorous pro-competitive policy has not been evident in the past.

COMPETITIVE ADVANTAGE AND THE SMALL FIRM

The industry/market characteristics outlined above constitute the market context in which firms compete. To greater or lesser degrees markets exhibit characteristics which inhibit firms from competing effectively – these are a joint product of the market-place and the firm's difficulty in deploying its resources effectively. This section looks briefly at some of the difficulties viewed from the supply side (the small firm) with some examples drawn from small 'high-tech' firms.

Competitive advantage arises from the value a firm is able to create for its customers over and above the firm's cost of creating that advantage. 'Competitive strategy' as a generic strategy specifies a fundamental approach to achieving the competitive advantage a firm is pursuing. Thus, a firm may be aiming to be a low-cost producer (the generic strategy) and it might aim to achieve this primarily by achieving economies of scale in its assembly operations and secondarily by adopting minimum cost, efficiency-based procedures throughout its operations.

In putting into effect its competitive strategy (see Figure 8.2) the most critical choices exhibited by a firm are concerned with the selection of the product market areas or segments in which the firm will compete and the resource deployments which serve these segments. Product market choices represent the 'scope' of the firm's activities (Teece 1980). Resource deployment represents the firm's attempt to create idiosyncratic capital which, by definition, cannot be readily imitated without high cost and/or significant risk. It is the profitable juxtaposition of idiosyncratic capital against product markets that is the essence of the firm's strategic task (Rumelt 1981). One of the essential characteristics of the 'successful' firm is therefore its distinctiveness relative to its competitors in terms of its underlying assets, both tangible and intangible (Stasch and Ward 1985; Woo and Cooper 1985).

These assets are reflected in the cost structure of the firm, or – as Porter (1985) has popularized it – in the value chain. The value chain focuses attention on the identification of the elements of the cost structure and the underlying variables which determine its behaviour. Management of the individual elements of cost and

Figure 8.2: Competitive strategy. Source: I am indebted to Michael Gould for the original version of this figure.

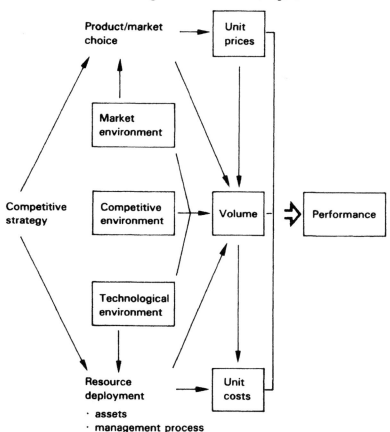

the interfaces between these elements of costs create 'value'. The firm's assets lie behind the cost structure and by comparing cost structures across firms it is possible to identify the distinctive assets of a firm.

A broad dichotomy between 'simple' and 'complex' businesses can help in understanding the problems faced by a small firm. A 'simple' business is one where competitive advantage arises from doing one thing better than anyone else – e.g., having access to low-cost raw materials (e.g. high-purity Australian iron ore) or lower-cost labour, or a specific product designed by the owner-manager. Complex businesses are typically higher value added. Superior performance depends on doing a number of things well

189

and being able to co-ordinate and manage complex interactions between the different elements in the cost structure. Williamson (1970) and Williamson and Bhargava (1972) suggest some relevant theory and Steer and Cable (1978) offer some statistical evidence that organizational form does matter.

Although 'small firms' are far from being a homogeneous entity, a number of general propositions can be advanced:

(i) Small firms tend to be simple businesses.

(ii) Growth imposes considerable costs in terms of:

(a) developing new resources;

(b) creating more appropriate management processes.

(iii) These costs are greater the more complex the environment (market, competitors, technology) because of the necessity to create a distinctive position.

(iv) Low-cost expansion paths lack distinctiveness and create 'me-too' products.

(v) Barriers to entry and exercise of market power will inhibit growth by raising the costs of expansion and diversification.

These propositions can be refined and adjusted to suit particular market situations. The underlying proposition that growth requires new product-market choices, development of new specific assets, and major changes in management structure and process holds across a wide range of 'innovatory' environments.

It may well be the case and is a matter for empirical investigation that the threshold size at which some of these transitional costs become markedly lower in relation to size is significantly higher than the kinds of absolute size limits conventionally used to describe 'small' firms. If this were the case, it would mean that there are major managerial costs attached to even quite large firms in high-growth industries. It raises the question as to who does capture the real growth in high-growth industries, and (probably more important) who gains market share when the industry starts to mature.

Some interesting evidence is available from recent research on the development and growth of small 'high-tech' firms (Slatter 1987). Some of the propositions advanced include:

(i) Early growth often hides major strategic weaknesses. The firm's skill base is often extremely narrow which means that new growth can be like a new start-up – with all the same risks. This

190

usually means that many small companies have a limited scope for development beyond their initial product market base. In addition the start-up position may inhibit development if the initial technology and market are too narrow or too mature.

(ii) Few firms are able to repeat their early success in designing and launching innovative products. Most firms' subsequent products are only incrementally better than those of their competitors and many firms resort to 'me-too' or 'easy-to-copy' products in an attempt to grow. Firms often move into mature markets with 'me-too' products where competition is already heavy.

(iii) Successful development strategies are based on:

(a) being seen to be 'specialists';

(b) continuous and concerted effort to differentiate thereby avoiding head-on competition with large firms;

(c) deliberate, planned attempts to grow and diversify with careful attention to the product market choice and the resource base.

(iv) Supplier relationships are an important constraint. Many firms have to buy products and components from large overseas suppliers. US semiconductor companies, for example, require very long lead times. The cost of up-front cash payments to obtain semi-customized chips (for example) are a recurring problem. Limited cash resources mean that firms often have to settle for standard chips which result in 'me-too' products.

In this brief examination of the strategic choices facing small firms we see two concepts which are at the heart of business strategy but which are neglected in neo-classical theory – the concepts of enterpreneurship (which I have not expanded upon) and of resource heterogeneity. Resource heterogeneity is an endogenous creation of economic actors. Without resource heterogeneity and the equivalent of property rights to unique resources there is little incentive to invest in the risky exploration of new methods and the search for new value. Industries differ, in the standard view, according to the degree of concentration, the presence of scale economies, and the degree of product differentiation. Scale economies and product differentiation are viewed in this framework as properties of the industry rather than as results achieved by firms, and both are identified as barriers to entry creating economic rents for all firms in the industry. Thus, market power is an asset shared by all firms. But firms are clearly not alike and follow different strategies with respect to degree of vertical integration and product-market choice. Thus, in addition to the industry-wide factors which condition entry, there exist firm-specific factors which account for intra-industry differences in performance. Competition (intra-industry) is therefore a reflection of these firm-specific factors, and one must take care to distinguish between generic industry characteristics which may shape the rules of the game, and the ability of firms to change the rules of the game (if only marginally) in their favour.

CONCLUSION

The weight of the evidence on market structure and the competitive positioning of small firms suggests that the really systematic and pervasive problems faced by small firms are internal to the firm, such as the technical skill base, the management systems and processes, appropriate organization structures, and the availability of skilled managers. In terms of positioning the firm against the market, small firms are specially handicapped by their limited resources and the restricted range of assets they have available. Therefore they have difficulties in expanding simultaneously on technical, product, market, organizational, and managerial fronts.

External factors are clearly important to small firms if only because of the natural advantages enjoyed by larger competitors. There is no conclusive evidence that small firms are systematically disadvantaged by the exercise of market power by oligopolists except in some specific and fairly obvious instances. There are grounds for concern about the weak bargaining power of small firms with large buyers and with large overseas suppliers particularly. Finally, there is some generalized concern with the consequences of merger activity, its effect on aggregate concentration, and the implications for small firms.

REFERENCES

Aaronovitch, S. and Sawyer, M. (1975) *Big Business: Theoretical and Empirical Aspects of Concentration and Mergers in the UK*, London: Macmillan.

Baden Fuller (1982) private communication based on the research programme 'Strategies in mature industries in Europe' at the Centre for Business Strategy, London: London Business School.

Bannock, G. (1981) *The Economics of Small Business: Return from the Wilderness*, Oxford: Basil Blackwell.

Bolton (1971) *Small Firms: Report of the Committee of Inquiry on Small Firms*, London: HMSO.

Boston Consulting Group (1968) *Perspectives on Experience*, Boston: The Boston Consulting Group.

Boston Consulting Group (1974) *Perspectives on Experience*, Boston: The Boston Consulting Group.

Buzzell, R.D. and Wiersema, F.D. (1981) 'Successful share-building strategies', *Harvard Business Review*, Jan.–Feb.: 135–44.

Davies, I.R. and Kelly, M. (1972) *Small Firms in the Manufacturing Sector*, Committee of Enquiry on Small Firms Research Report No. 3, London: HMSO.

Edwards, C.D. (1964) Hearings before the sub-committee on antitrust and monopoly of the Committee of the Judiciary of the United States Senate, Part 1: overall and conglomerate aspects, Washington.

Fitzroy, P.T. (1985) 'Effects of buyer/seller concentration on profitability', in Thomas, H. and Gardner, D. (eds), *Strategic Marketing and Management*, Chichester: Wiley.

Galbraith, J.K. (1957) *American Capitalism, The Concept of Countervailing Power*, London: Hamish Hamilton.

Gale, B.T. (1972) 'Market share and rate of return', *Review of Economics and Statistics* 54(4): 412–23.

Ganguly, P. (1985) *UK Small Business Statistics and International Comparisons*, London: Harper & Row.

Ghazanfar, A. (1984) 'An analysis of competition in the office reprographics industry in the UK 1880–1980', PhD thesis, University of London.

Grant, R. (1985) 'Birds Eye and the UK frozen food industry: case study', London Business School.

Hall, W.K. (1980) 'Survival strategies in a hostile environment', *Harvard Business Review*, Sept.–Oct.: 75–85.

Hamermesh, R.G., Anderson, M.J., and Harris, E.J. (1978) 'Strategies for low market share businesses', *Harvard Business Review* 56(3): 95–102.

Hamermesh, R.G. and Silk, S.B. (1979) 'How to compete in stagnant industries', *Harvard Business Review* Sept.–Oct.: 161–68.

Hannah, L. and Kay, J.A. (1977) *Concentration in Modern Industry: Theory, Measurement, and the UK Experience*, London: Macmillan.

HMSO (1966) *An Approach to Industrial Strategy*, White Paper, Cmnd 6315.

HMSO (1978) *A Review of Monopolies and Mergers Policy*, Cmnd 7198.

Hofer, C.W. and Davoust, M.J. (1977) *Successful Strategic Management*, Chicago: A.T. Kearney.

Imel, B. and Helmberger, P. (1971) 'Estimation of structure–profit relations with application to the food-processing sector', *American Economic Review* 61 (Sept.): 614–27.

Kitching, J. (1967) 'Why do mergers miscarry?' *Harvard Business Review* Nov.–Dec.

Leavitt, T. (1980) 'Marketing success through differentiation – of anything', *Harvard Business Review* Jan.–Feb.: 83–91.

Leontiades, M. (1986) *Managing the Unmanageable: Strategies for Success within the Conglomerate*, Reading Mass.: Addison-Wesley.

Levicki, C. (ed.) (1984) *Small Business: Theory and Policy*, Beckenham: Croom Helm.

Lustgarten, S.H. (1975) 'The impact of buyer concentration in manufacturing industries', *Review of Economics and Statistics* 62(2): 125–32.

Mayer, K. (1947) 'Small business as a social institution', *Social Research* 14(3) September.

McGee, J., Ashe, G., and Jowett, P. (1986) 'The software industry in the UK', working paper, Alvey Directorate, Department of Trade and Industry.

McGee, J., Ghazanfar, A., and Thomas, H. (1986) 'The impact of technological change on industry structure and corporate strategy: the case of the office reprographics industry in the UK', working paper MRP86/87, Oxford: Templeton College.

McGee, J. and Thomas, H. (1986) 'Strategic groups: theory, research, and taxonomy', *Strategic Management Journal* 7: 141–60.

Meeks, G. (1977) *Disappointing Marriage: A Study of the Gains from Merger*, Cambridge: Cambridge University Press.

NEDC (1970) 'Memorandum of evidence', unpublished, reported in Davies and Kelly (1972).

Office of Fair Trading (1985a) *Annual Report of the Director General of the Office of Fair Trading*, London: HMSO.

PIMS (1977) *Selected Findings From the PIMS Program*, Cambridge, Mass.: The Strategic Planning Institute.

Porter, M.E. (1985) *Competitive Advantage*, New York: Free Press.

Prahalad, C.K. and Hamel, G. (1985) 'Do you really have a global strategy?', *Harvard Business Review* July–August.

Prais, S.J. (1976) *The Evolution of Giant Firms in the United Kingdom*, Cambridge: Cambridge University Press.

Prais, S.K. (1981) *Productivity and Industrial Structure*, Cambridge: Cambridge University Press.

Rumelt, R.P. (1974) *Strategy, Structure and Economic Performance*, Division of Research, Harvard University Graduate School of Business Administration.

Rumelt, R.P. (1981) 'Towards a strategic theory of the firm', working paper, University of Southern California.

Salter, M.S. and Weinhold, W.A. (1979) *Diversification Through Acquisition: Strategies for Creating Economic Value*, New York: Free Press.

Sawyer, M.C. (1981) *The Economics of Industries and Firms*, Beckenham: Croom Helm.

Scherer, F.M., Beckenstein, A., Kaufer, E., and Murphy, R.D. (1975) *The Economics of Multi-Mart Operation – an International Comparison Study*, Cambridge, Mass.: Harvard University Press.

Scherer, F.M. (1980) *Industrial Market Structure and Economic Performance*, Chicago: Rand McNally.

Shepherd, W. (1972) 'The elements of market structure', *Review of Economics and Statistics* 54(1): 25–37.

Slatter, S. (1984) 'Management issues and problems of small high-tech firms: pilot study findings', Coopers and Lybrand High Tech Management Unit, London Business School.

Stanworth, J., Westrip, A., Watkins, D., and Lewis, J. (1982) *Perspectives on a Decade of Small Business Research*, Aldershot: Gower.

Stasch, S.F. and Ward, J.C. (1985) 'Growth strategies for small-share firms in mature industries', in Thomas, H. and Gardner, D. (eds) *Strategic Marketing and Management*, Chichester: Wiley.

Steer, P. and Cable, J. (1978) 'Internal organization and profit: an empirical analysis of large UK companies', *Journal of Industrial Economies* XXVII (1), September.

Strategic Planning Institute (1979) *Selected Findings from the PIMS Program*, Cambridge, Mass.: Strategic Planning Institute.

Teece, D.J. (1980) 'Economies of scope and the scope of the enterprise', *Journal of Economic Behaviour and Organization* 1: 223–47.

Thomas, H. and Gardner, D. (eds) (1985) *Strategic Marketing and Management*, Chichester: Wiley.

Utton, M.A. (1984) 'Concentration, competition and the small firm', in Levicki (ed.), *Small Business: Theory and Policy*, Beckenham: Croom Helm.

Ward, J.L. and Stasch, S.F. (1980b) 'Critical questions second-tier firms should ask before becoming aggressive in mature markets', Proceedings, American Marketing Association's Educators Conference, August: 206–8.

Williamson, O.E. (1970) *Corporate Control and Business Behaviour*, New Jersey: Prentice Hall.

Williamson, O.E. and Bhargava, N. (1972) 'Assessing and classifying the internal structure and control apparatus of the modern corporation, in Cowling, K.G. (ed.) *Market Structure and Corporate Behaviour*, London: Gray-Mills.

Woo, C.Y. and Cooper, A.C. (1979) 'Strategies of effective low-market share businesses', working paper, Purdue University, Krannert School of Business.

Woo, C.Y. and Cooper, A.C. (1981) 'Strategies for effective low-market share businesses', *Strategic Management Journal* 2(3) (July–September) 301–18.

Woo, C.Y. and Cooper, A.C. (1985) 'Corporate settings of effective low-share businesses', in Thomas, H. and Gardner, D. (eds) *Strategic Marketing and Management*, Chichester: Wiley.

Index